OECD Public Governance Reviews

The Regulation of Lobbying in Quebec, Canada

STRENGTHENING A CULTURE OF TRANSPARENCY AND INTEGRITY

This work is published under the responsibility of the Secretary-General of the OECD. The opinions expressed and arguments employed herein do not necessarily reflect the official views of the Member countries of the OECD.

This document, as well as any data and map included herein, are without prejudice to the status of or sovereignty over any territory, to the delimitation of international frontiers and boundaries and to the name of any territory, city or area.

The statistical data for Israel are supplied by and under the responsibility of the relevant Israeli authorities. The use of such data by the OECD is without prejudice to the status of the Golan Heights, East Jerusalem and Israeli settlements in the West Bank under the terms of international law.

Please cite this publication as:
OECD (2022), *The Regulation of Lobbying in Quebec, Canada: Strengthening a Culture of Transparency and Integrity*, OECD Public Governance Reviews, OECD Publishing, Paris, https://doi.org/10.1787/ec0cfef3-en.

ISBN 978-92-64-47169-6 (print)
ISBN 978-92-64-90785-0 (pdf)

OECD Public Governance Reviews
ISSN 2219-0406 (print)
ISSN 2219-0414 (online)

Photo credits: Cover © Emmanuel Coveney.

Corrigenda to publications may be found on line at: www.oecd.org/about/publishing/corrigenda.htm.
© OECD 2022

The use of this work, whether digital or print, is governed by the Terms and Conditions to be found at https://www.oecd.org/termsandconditions.

Foreword

Lobbying is a legitimate act of political participation and grants all interested stakeholders a right of access to the development and implementation of public policies. However, a fair and equitable framework for lobbying remains essential to promote transparency in policy-making processes and ensure inclusive and informed decision-making, while minimising the risk that public policies respond only to the needs of a few special interest groups. Rules and guidelines on lobbying are also instrumental in fostering citizen's trust in policymaking and reinforcing democracy, a key priority of the OECD.

In 2002, Quebec (Canada) adopted the Lobbying Transparency and Ethics Act, which remains one of the most comprehensive pieces of legislation among OECD countries. Nearly twenty years after its entry into force, reforms could help align the Act with best practices on transparency of influence communications as well as the main international standards on the regulation of lobbying.

The first purpose of this report is to provide an analysis of the legal and regulatory framework in place to strengthen transparency and integrity of lobbying practices in Quebec (Canada), as well as assess the reform project proposed by the Québec Commissioner of Lobbying in 2019, by situating it relation to the OECD Recommendation on Principles for Transparency and Integrity in Lobbying. Second, this report identifies concrete solutions and good practices implemented in OECD countries that could be adapted to the Quebec context.

By considering the recommendations proposed in this report, Quebec could encourage further political and civic dialogue on how to modernise the legislative and regulatory framework in order to strengthen a culture of transparency and integrity of lobbying in Quebec.

This document [GOV/PGC/INT(2022)2] was approved by the OECD Working Party of Senior Public Integrity Officials (SPIO) on 15 March 2022 and prepared for publication by the OECD Secretariat.

Acknowledgements

The present report was drafted by the OECD Public Governance Directorate (GOV) under the leadership of Elsa Pilichowski, Director. It was coordinated and drafted by Pauline Bertrand and Frédéric Boehm, under the supervision of Julio Bacio Terracino, Head of the Public Sector Integrity Division in GOV. The report was prepared for publication by Meral Gedik, with administrative support of Aman Johal and Balazs Gyimesi.

The OECD thanks the Quebec Commissioner of Lobbying and the Ministry of International Relations and La Francophonie of Quebec for their support throughout the project.

The OECD expresses its gratitude to all stakeholders who took part in discussions organised as part of the fact-finding mission that took place from 7 to 24 September 2021. This report benefited from discussions with representatives of Quebec government and municipal institutions: the Treasury Board Secretariat, the Ministry of Municipal Affairs and Housing, the Ministry of the Environment and the Fight Against Climate Change, the Ministry of Transport, the Ministry of Finance, the Ministry for Health and Social Services, the Ministry of Energy and Natural Resources, the Ministry of Agriculture, the Ministry of Agriculture, Fisheries and Food, the Autorité des marchés financiers, the Autorité des marchés publics, the Régie des alcools, des courses et des jeux, Hydro-Québec, the Ethics Commissioner, Élections Québec, the City of Laval's Office of Integrity and Ethics, as well as institutions in the health and social services (CHU Québec, CIUSSS Mauricie – Centre du Québec, CISSS Gaspésie – Îles-de-la-Madeleine, Centre d'approvisionnement gouvernemental). The OECD also thanks the parliamentary and municipal elected officials, organisations representing municipalities (Union des Municipalités du Québec, Fédération québécoise des municipalités, Association des Directeurs Généraux des Municipalités du Québec), civil society organisations, private sector representatives, journalists, researchers and members of the Commission of Inquiry on the Awarding and Management of Public Contracts in the Construction Industry who participated in these interviews for their significant contributions.

Table of contents

Foreword	3
Acknowledgements	4
Executive summary	7
1 A legislative and regulatory framework adapted to the socio-political and administrative context of Quebec	**9**
Introduction	10
Modernising the legal framework to promote the emergence of a consensus on the legitimacy of lobbying in Quebec	15
Adapting the scope of the law to the different local levels and taking into account existing regulatory frameworks	19
Provide in the law a robust definition of the terms "lobbying" and "lobbyist" adapted to local realities and the changing lobbying landscape	33
References	52
Notes	55
2 An approach to transparency of lobbying activities based on the relevance of the information declared	**57**
Introduction	58
Clarify registration and disclosure procedures for all actors involved	58
Strengthening the content of information reported to the register	64
Maximising the technological environment of the Lobbyists Registry as a vehicle for transparency and accountability	74
Sharing responsibility for transparency with public decision-makers	79
Implementing mechanisms for effective implementation and enforcement of disclosure obligations	81
Enabling an effective review of the Act	87
References	90
Note	91
3 Promote a culture of integrity in the interactions between public officials and lobbyists in Quebec	**93**
Introduction	94
Strengthening the integrity framework for public officials	94
Promoting responsible engagement of lobbyists	104
References	108
Annex A. Statement of Principles of the Québec Commissioner of Lobbying (2019)	109

FIGURES

Figure 1.1. Trust in institutions remains volatile in Canada	11
Figure 1.2. The policy-making process	20
Figure 1.3. Lobbying regulations targeting local governments in OECD countries	23
Figure 1.4. Ministers and Members of Parliament are usually covered by the requirements of lobbying regulations	33
Figure 2.1. Best means for regulating lobbying, according to lobbyists	65
Figure 2.2. In OECD countries, lobbyists favour disclosure of political campaigns contributions when registering lobbying activities	65
Figure 3.1. More standards are needed for public officials on their interactions with lobbyists	95

TABLES

Table 1.1. Changes in the scope of the Lobbying Transparency and Ethics Act (2002)	13
Table 1.2. Principles on which to base a lobbying legislation (Delphi study)	16
Table 1.3. Terminology proposed by the Quebec Commissioner of Lobbying in its Statement of Principles	17
Table 1.4. Alternative terminologies used in international lobbying legislations	18
Table 1.5. Risks of undue influence along the policy cycle	21
Table 1.6. Regulatory framework for awarding public contracts in Quebec	29
Table 1.7. Lobbyists subject to the Lobbying Transparency and Ethics Act	34
Table 1.8. Actors subject to transparency requirements in their lobbying activities	37
Table 1.9. Nomenclature of collective action organisations in Quebec	40
Table 2.1. Registration deadlines in Canadian provinces and some municipalities	60
Table 2.2. Who undertakes lobbying activities, on what and how?	67
Table 2.3. Updating and renewal of the information of the initial return in Quebec	68
Table 2.4. Frequency of disclosure of communications and meetings between lobbyists and public officials in selected countries	69
Table 2.5. Monitoring of representations made to elected or designated officials in Canadian jurisdictions with lobbying legislations in place	70
Table 2.6. Structure and number of employees of the Quebec Commissioner of Lobbying	83
Table 2.7. Criminal sanctions for breaches of the Act's obligations	84
Table 2.8. Awareness actions carried out by the Quebec Commissioner of Lobbying	87

Follow OECD Publications on:

http://twitter.com/OECD_Pubs

http://www.facebook.com/OECDPublications

http://www.linkedin.com/groups/OECD-Publications-4645871

http://www.youtube.com/oecdilibrary

http://www.oecd.org/oecddirect/

Executive summary

In 2002, Quebec adopted the *Lobbying Transparency and Ethics Act*. This Act recognises the legitimacy of lobbying and the right of citizens to know who is attempting to influence decision-makers in parliamentary, government and municipal institutions. It provides for the mandatory registration of lobbyists in a public registry, a code of conduct applicable to those who engage in lobbying activities, a Commissioner of Lobbying responsible for the monitoring and oversight of these activities, and a system of criminal and disciplinary sanctions.

In order to respond to changing lobbying practices and the evolving socio-political context in Quebec, Quebec could consider modernising the legislative and regulatory framework to continue strengthening a culture of transparency and integrity.

Main findings

In Quebec, the same legal and institutional framework applies to both lobbying activities targeting the Quebec government and activities taking place at the municipal level. In this respect, the Lobbying Transparency and Ethics Act is one of the most comprehensive and coherent legislative frameworks among OECD countries, and it is therefore desirable to maintain its coverage of municipalities. However, this specificity requires finding a balance between the Act's objective of transparency, addressing risks in local public management, and the proper functioning of local democracy, for example the need to maintain a citizen dialogue with public institutions.

The Quebec legislator made a choice in 2002 to apply transparency requirements to actors based on whether their activities involve the pursuit of a pecuniary and corporate benefit, rather than on the nature of their influence communications and their impact on public decision-making. However, these criteria are insufficiently clear and can be seen as hindering transparency. Above all, this categorisation may have contributed to perceptions that only certain activities carried out for corporate interests should be associated with the word "lobbying" and be subject to legislative measures to prevent abuse. Today, lobbying in Quebec is perceived negatively by the public and remains associated with certain practices that may be considered illegitimate or even illegal.

The reporting obligations in the Lobbyist Registry only imperfectly meet the transparency objectives of the Act and do not allow for a real understanding of the scope or weight of a lobbying activity. The launch in the spring of 2022 by the Quebec Commissioner of Lobbying of a new platform designed to remedy the technological shortcomings of the current Registry will undoubtedly constitute an important step towards greater simplicity and efficiency in relation to transparency obligations.

Despite the Quebec Commissioner of Lobbying's extensive awareness-raising activities, the benefits of a lobbying framework are not sufficiently known to the public. Moreover, the Act does not clearly assign responsibilities to the State, public institutions and public office holders with respect to the transparency of lobbying activities.

Main recommendations

While maintaining the coverage of the current Act with respect to municipalities, the Quebec legislator could consider further adapting the scope of application to different local levels and types of decisions. Similarly, the Act could better reflect advances in transparency and integrity made possible by the Act respecting contracting by public bodies and the strengthening of electoral laws.

In order to take into account the evolution of lobbying practices, made more complex by the advent of social media, the Act could cover grassroots lobbying, as is the case at the federal level and in most Canadian jurisdictions. The Act should also consider the definition of "lobbyist" in an inclusive manner to cover all interest groups, whether business or not-for-profit entities, that seek to influence public decisions. However, in order to strike the right balance between the diversity of lobbying entities, their capacities and resources, on the one hand, and the measures taken to increase transparency, on the other hand, it seems necessary to provide for exemptions for certain collective action organisations and *ad hoc* lobbying activities. These measures appear necessary so that the administrative burden of compliance does not become an impediment to fair and equitable access to government.

The provisions regarding the "significant part of duties" is confusing and could be reviewed. At the very least, the Quebec legislator could consider providing that the status of lobbyist is assessed by considering all of the activities of the legal person concerned, and not those of the individuals who make up the entity, in order to determine more relevant thresholds triggering an obligation to register.

The register should place the obligation to register on entities, not individuals. The initial declaration could be simplified, while more precise information -- such as the dates of lobbying activities, the specific public officials and decisions targeted -- could be required in regular updates, in order to allow citizens to fully grasp the scope and depth of these activities. These measures could be complemented by tailored disclosures according to the category of public official targeted.

Public officials and lobbyists share the responsibility to apply the principles of good governance, in particular transparency and integrity, in order to maintain confidence in public decisions. On the lobbyists' side, the Code of conduct could be strengthened and Quebec could encourage companies and interest representatives to implement principles of responsible engagement. On the part of public officials, the regulation of lobbying activities must also be part of a broader approach aimed at promoting a culture of integrity within public institutions. Quebec could consider making public officials partly accountable by requiring them to ensure that representatives of companies or organisations contacting them have actually registered their lobbying activities, or by implementing open agenda initiatives for certain public officials. Increased co-ordination with the Treasury Board Secretariat of Quebec, the Ethics Commissioner of Quebec and the Municipal Commission of Quebec on matters related to lobbying and integrity could help strengthen awareness and promote training activities on the integrity standards applicable to public officials in the specific context of lobbying activities.

Finally, to ensure compliance with the rules, the Quebec legislator could consider giving the Commissioner of Lobbying the power to impose administrative monetary penalties, as well an educational mission to raise awareness so as to reinforce the efforts already made by the Commissioner in this area.

1 A legislative and regulatory framework adapted to the socio-political and administrative context of Quebec

This chapter analyses the legislative and regulatory framework set up by Quebec to address the governance concerns related to lobbying practices. First, the chapter provides avenues of consideration to modernise the legal framework in terms of its objectives and terminology, in order to foster the emergence of a consensus on the legitimacy of lobbying in Quebec. The chapter also discusses how the scope of the law could be adapted at different local levels and be consistent with the wider policy and regulatory frameworks. Lastly, the chapter provides concrete recommendations to strengthen the definitions of the terms "lobbying" and "lobbyist" so that they are adapted to various local realities and to the evolving lobbying landscape.

Introduction

Lobbying[1] in all its forms, including advocacy and other methods of influencing public policy, is a legitimate act of political participation. It gives relevant actors and all interested stakeholders a right of access to the development and implementation of public policies. All interest groups, be they companies, non-profit organisations, think tanks or trade associations, represent legitimate interests and provide public officials with expertise, technical knowledge, useful data and much-needed insights on all matters of public interest. This information from a diversity of interests and stakeholders enables an inclusive policy-making process that leads to better and ultimately more informed policies. It is also a key incentive for public authorities to take up and address certain social or societal issues. Lastly, consulting with relevant stakeholders before any public decision is taken or a given standard is adopted allows for greater acceptance of the latter afterwards (OECD, 2021[1]).

However, experience shows that policy-making processes are not always inclusive and can lead to situations of undue influence and/or monopoly of influence. At times, influence may be concentrated in the hands of those that are financially and politically powerful, to the detriment of those who have fewer resources (monopoly of influence). This imbalance can exacerbate disadvantages of groups with fewer resources and less capacities to engage in formulating policy. Experience also shows that public policies can be unduly influenced through the provision of biased or deceitful evidence or data, or by manipulating public opinion (undue influence). Studies increasingly show that lobbying practices, when they take place outside of transparency and integrity frameworks, and when they involve only a small group of stakeholders, lead to a misallocation of public resources, lower productivity and the perpetuation of social inequalities (OECD, 2017[2])

These situations have the potential to undermine trust in public authorities and in those who influence the policy-making process, particularly businesses. Indeed, in Quebec, the extent of the corruption and undue influence schemes exposed before the Commission of Inquiry on the Awarding and Management of Public Contracts in the Construction Industry (the Charbonneau Commission) had already seriously undermined public confidence in government institutions (Commission d'enquête sur l'octroi et la gestion des contrats publics dans l'industrie de la construction, 2015[3]; Bégin, Brodeur and Lalonde, 2016[4]).

Today, lobbying in Quebec is still perceived negatively by the general public and remains associated with certain practices that may be considered illegitimate. The Canadian results of the Edelman Trust Barometer 2021 reveal, for example, that 50% of Canadian respondents worry that business leaders are purposely trying to mislead them and 46% believe the same about government leaders (Edelman, 2021[5]). These results also show that trust in government, businesses, non-governmental organisations (NGOs) and the media remains volatile in Canada (Figure 1.1).

Figure 1.1. Trust in institutions remains volatile in Canada

Percentage of Canadian respondents who trust the following institutions

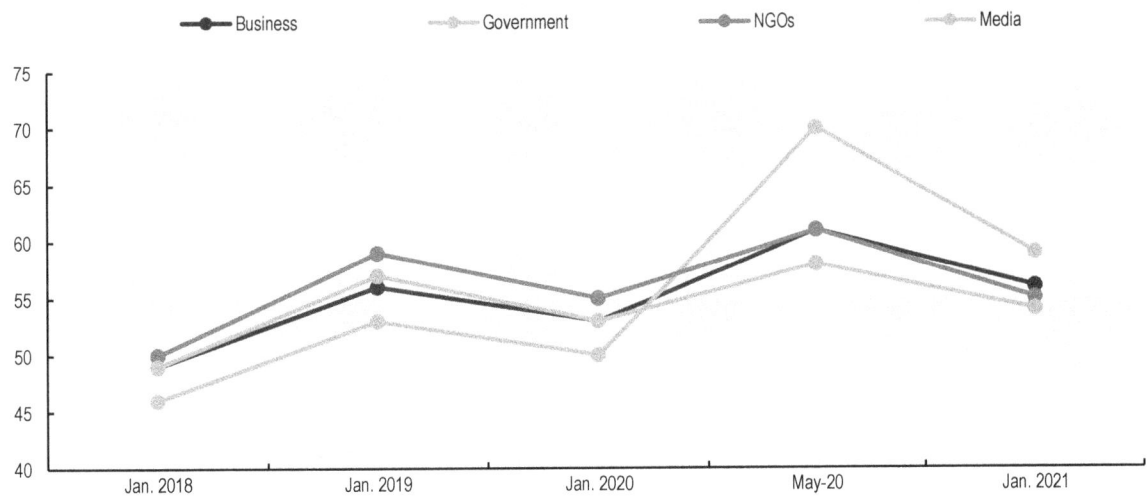

Source: (Edelman, 2021[5])

For this reason, the OECD Recommendation on Principles for Transparency and Integrity in Lobbying (hereinafter referred to as "the Recommendation"), adopted on 18 February 2010 by the OECD Council, provides international guidelines for governments to address risks of undue influence as well as inequity in the power of influence (OECD, 2010[6]). The Recommendation provides directions and guidance on how to promote equal access to policy discussions for all parties concerned, and how to enhance transparency, integrity and mechanisms for effective implementation, based on 10 principles and 4 key pillars. The Recommendation also reflects the views of a wide range of OECD bodies and stakeholders, including legislators, private sector representatives, lobbying associations, civil society organisations, trade unions, think tanks and international organisations (Box 1.1).

Furthermore, the Recommendation emphasises that the Principles are valid at both national and sub-national levels. Indeed, many significant public decisions on public services, such as social services, health care and education, the welfare system, as well as land use, housing, planning and infrastructure issues and environmental protection, are made at the subnational level, particularly in federal countries where significant decision-making powers reside in state or provincial governments. A strong framework for lobbying at the sub-national level is therefore key when pursuing the objective of transparency and integrity of decision-making processes.

> **Box 1.1. OECD Principles for Transparency and Integrity in Lobbying (extract)**
>
> **I. Building an effective and fair framework for openness and access**
>
> 1. Countries should provide a level playing field by granting all stakeholders fair and equitable access to the development and implementation of public policies.
> 2. Rules and guidelines on lobbying should address the governance concerns related to lobbying practices, and respect the socio-political and administrative contexts.
> 3. Rules and guidelines on lobbying should be consistent with the wider policy and regulatory frameworks
> 4. Countries should clearly define the terms 'lobbying' and 'lobbyist' when they consider or develop rules and guidelines on lobbying.
>
> **II. Enhancing transparency**
>
> 5. Countries should provide an adequate degree of transparency to ensure that public officials, citizens and businesses can obtain sufficient information on lobbying activities.
> 6. Countries should enable stakeholders – including civil society organisations, businesses, the media and the general public – to scrutinise lobbying activities.
>
> **III. Fostering a culture of integrity**
>
> 7. Countries should foster a culture of integrity in public organisations and decision making by providing clear rules and guidelines of conduct for public officials.
> 8. Lobbyists should comply with standards of professionalism and transparency; they share responsibility for fostering a culture of transparency and integrity in lobbying.
>
> **IV. Mechanisms for effective implementation, compliance and review**
>
> 9. Countries should involve key actors in implementing a coherent spectrum of strategies and practices to achieve compliance.
> 10. Countries should review the functioning of their rules and guidelines related to lobbying on a periodic basis and make necessary adjustments in light of experience.
>
> Source: For the full text see OECD/LEGAL/0379

The Recommendation has proven valuable in its ability to inform policy debates at the national and sub-national levels in jurisdictions that are adopting or revising regulations or measures on lobbying. This is notably the case in Quebec. Indeed, the Quebec Commissioner of Lobbying[2], the independent public authority responsible for ensuring compliance with the legal framework on lobbying, used the principles included in the Recommendation to assess the implementation of the 2002 Quebec Lobbying Transparency and Ethics Act (hereafter "the Act") (Légis Québec, 2002[7]). This Act recognises the legitimacy of lobbying and the right of the public to know who is trying to influence decision-makers of parliamentary, government and municipal institutions. It provides for the mandatory registration of lobbyists in a public registry, a code of conduct applicable to those who engage in lobbying activities, a Commissioner of Lobbying responsible for the monitoring and control of these activities, and a system of penal and disciplinary sanctions (Lobbyisme Québec, 2019[8]). Several legislative and regulatory texts have since specified its scope of application (Table 1.1).

Table 1.1. Changes in the scope of the Lobbying Transparency and Ethics Act (2002)

Law / regulation	Year of adoption	Main changes made
Lobbying Transparency and Ethics Act Exclusions Regulation	2002	Lobbying activities on behalf of an association or other non-profit group not constituted to serve management, union or professional interests, nor composed of a majority of members that are profit-seeking enterprises or representatives of profit-seeking enterprises, are not covered by the law.
Code of Conduct for Lobbyists	2004	Complementary to the Act, the Code sets out standards of conduct and values to which lobbyists must adhere in their communications with public decision-makers (elected officials or civil servants): respect for institutions, honesty, integrity, professionalism. Non-compliance with the Code renders a lobbyist liable to penalties.
Act to modify the organisation and governance of the health and social services network, in particular by abolishing the regional agencies	2015	Lobbying activities carried out towards health institutions merged into Integrated Health and Social Services Centres (CISSS) and Integrated University Health and Social Services Centres (CIUSSS), as well as with certain non-merged institutions, must be registered in the Lobbyists Registry.
Bill No. 6: An Act to transfer responsibility for the registry of lobbyists to the Lobbyists Commissioner and to implement the Charbonneau Commission recommendation on the prescription period for bringing penal proceedings	2019	The Act gives the Quebec Commissioner of Lobbying the responsibility to administer the Lobbyists Registry, which was previously entrusted to the Personal and Movable Real Rights Registry Office within the Ministry of Justice, who acted as Registrar of the Lobbyists Registry. The Act also provides for the extension of the prescription period applicable to penal proceedings.

Source: OECD, based on information communicated by the Quebec Commissioner of Lobbying.

In June 2019, the Commissioner of Lobbying tabled a report in the Quebec National Assembly proposing the adoption of a complete overhaul of the Lobbying Transparency and Ethics Act (Lobbyisme Québec, 2019[8]). The report benefited from extensive consultations with experts, elected representatives of parliament and municipalities, heads of departments and agencies, and representatives of businesses and organisations. Focus groups were also organised on behalf of the Commissioner to better understand the perceptions of lobbying and the expectations of citizens with regard to its regulation.

On the one hand, the report establishes a diagnosis of the Act regulating lobbying in Quebec and proposes an analysis of the various conceptual, operational and technical challenges related to the application of the Act since it came into force in 2002. The report considers that the Act has become ill adapted to the evolution of the socio-political context, presents serious problems of understanding and application, and is deficient in the achievement of its democratic objectives. In addition, there are multiple contextual, conceptual and operational problems in the interpretation and application of the Act (Box 1.2).

> **Box 1.2. Main contextual, conceptual and operational challenges identified in Commissioner of Lobbying's diagnosis**
>
> **Contextual challenges**
>
> The context of the emergence of the Act, adopted in response to a crisis, has paradoxically generated more distrust of lobbying by citizens and a stigmatisation of lobbyists. The legitimacy of lobbying remains insufficiently understood, while elected officials and public servants also show reluctance towards the provisions of the Act. Despite the Commissioner of Lobbying's awareness-raising work, the benefits of a lobbying regulation are not sufficiently known to foster public approval, as the Commissioner of Lobbying does not have a clear educational mission on the transparency and legitimacy of lobbying activities. The punitive and repressive dimension of the Act contributes to certain confusions between malpractice and lobbying. Finally, the regime is not adapted to the socio-political and institutional evolution of Quebec.
>
> **Conceptual challenges**
>
> The scope of the Act promotes the idea that there are "good" and "bad" lobbyists, and reinforces the divide between so-called "socially noble" objectives, which are perceived as legitimate, and the "mercantile" objectives that the Act should necessarily regulate. Indeed, some influence communications (non-monetary purposes) or lobbyist groups (non-profit organisations) do not fall within the scope of the Act, creating an inequality of treatment and a lack of transparency. The lack of clear definition of certain terms creates ambiguity, compromising the understanding and application of the Act. Finally, the Act does not clearly assign responsibilities to public institutions and officials, which has led to a detachment of some elected officials and staff of public institutions from the implementation of the Act.
>
> **Operational and technical challenges**
>
> Some concepts are confusing and criminal sanctions are inappropriate for the types of offences committed by lobbyists. Insufficient fines undermine the credibility of the Act. The information contained in lobbyists' disclosures does not provide a true understanding of the scope or relative weight of a lobbying activity.
>
> Source: (Lobbyisme Québec, 2019[8]).

On the other hand, the report proposes a statement of 34 principles for legislators (hereinafter "the Statement of Principles") for a complete overhaul of the current framework in order to better align it with best practices identified in the area of transparency of influence communications as well as with the main international standards on transparency of lobbying activities - including the OECD Recommendation (Annex A).

For several years, the Commissioner already expressed the wish to change the Lobbying Transparency and Ethics Act, and made proposals for legislative amendments to this effect (Lobbyisme Québec, 2008[9]; 2012[10]; 2016[11]; 2017[12]). The purpose of the 2019 report to the members of the National Assembly was to encourage a dialogue on the modernisation of the legislative and regulatory framework in order to foster the emergence of a consensus on the adoption of new legislation that would respond to the changes and challenges of lobbying in Quebec and further promote citizens' trust in public institutions.

This chapter analyses the scope of application of the Lobbying Transparency and Ethics Act. Specifically, it examines the notion of "lobbying" in Quebec's legal and regulatory framework, its scope in terms of the public decisions concerned, and the definitions of "lobbying" and "lobbyist".

Modernising the legal framework to promote the emergence of a consensus on the legitimacy of lobbying in Quebec

The *OECD Recommendation on Principles for Transparency and Integrity in Lobbying* encourages jurisdictions to provide a level playing field by granting all stakeholders fair and equitable access to the development and implementation of public policies (Principle 1 of the Recommendation). There are many ways to foster participation (OECD, 2017[13]), and the legal recognition of lobbying as a means of access to public policy making for all stakeholders from the private sector and the public at large is an essential component of promoting participation. This legal recognition also ensures a level playing field for interest groups, whether business or not-for-profit entities, which aim to influence public decisions. The Recommendation also states that countries should weigh all available regulatory and policy options to select an appropriate solution that addresses key concerns such as the level of public trust (Principle 2 of the Recommendation). In this perspective, the legal framework regulating lobbying in Quebec could be modernised:

- In its objectives pursued; and
- In the terminology used.

Article 1 of the Act could include a principle of fair access to public decision makers

In Quebec, the *Lobbying Transparency and Ethics Act* adopted in 2002 recognises in its Article 1 that lobbying is "a legitimate means of access to parliamentary, governmental and municipal institutions, and that it is in the interest of the public that it be able to know who is attempting to influence such institutions" (Légis Québec, 2002[7]). By enshrining the legitimacy of lobbying and the objective of transparency of lobbying activities, the Act has allowed Quebec to join a global trend of Canadian and international jurisdictions adopting legal frameworks for lobbying. Indeed, in 2020, 18 of the countries adhering to the OECD Recommendation had public registers containing information on lobbyists and/or lobbying activities. In these countries, the adoption of lobbying laws and regulations has been a key lever for legitimising these activities. All Canadian provinces and territories, with the exception of the Northwest Territories and Nunavut, have also adopted a specific framework recognising the legitimacy of interactions between public officials and lobbyists (OECD, 2021[1]).

To further strengthen the objectives of the Act, Quebec could include an objective of fair access to public decision-makers. Indeed, a single objective of transparency may suggest that these activities are necessarily marked by opacity and suspicion. The OECD Recommendation recalls in Principle 1 that gaining balanced perspectives on issues leads to informed policy debate and formulation of effective policies, and public officials should promote fair and equitable representation of business and societal interests. Allowing all stakeholders, from the private sector and the public at large, fair and equitable access to participate in the development of public policies is crucial to protect the integrity of decisions and to safeguard the public interest by counterbalancing vocal vested interests, and to foster citizens' trust in public decision making (Principle 1 of the Recommendation).

A study conducted by the Research Chair on Democracy and Parliamentary Institutions at Université Laval among three groups of stakeholders concerned with the regulation of lobbying (lobbyists, lobbying regulators and researchers) showed that the objective of equitable access to public decision-makers is agreed upon by the respondents (Ouimet, Montigny and Jacob, 2019[14]) (Table 1.2).

Table 1.2. Principles on which to base a lobbying legislation (Delphi study)

The experts responded to the following question: "Please assess the relevance of establishing a lobbying legislation on the following principles"

	Item covered by the Act and its regulations, or the Code of Ethics	Consensus (%) among lobbyists	Consensus (%) among lobbying regulators	Consensus (%) among researchers
Transparency	●	91.7%	100%	100%
Legitimacy of lobbying	●	85.3%	80%	78.6%
Relevance of information to the public	○	78.8%	100%	92.9%
Right to information	●	63.5%	60%	35.6%
Ethics and integrity	●	82.7%	90%	100%
Access to decision makers	●	94.2%	100%	100%
Equitable access to decision makers	○	85.3%	80%	92.9%
Shared responsibility between the lobbyist and the public office holder	○	85.3%	70%	71.4%
Accountability of the public office holder	○	80.1%	60%	57.1%
Professionalism	●	82.7%	90%	64.3%

● Covered
○ Not covered

Note: The categories of experts interviewed include lobbyists with recent experience of disclosure in the Quebec Lobbyists Registry, lobbying regulators in Canada, and researchers who have empirically studied lobbying regulation and its impacts. Consensus is considered strong when the relevance of a statement has been assessed by at least 75% of experts from at least two categories of experts examined in the study.
Source: (Ouimet, Montigny and Jacob, 2019[14]).

Including an objective of equitable access to public decision-makers would thus reinforce the objectives pursued by the legislator, and position the Act as a fundamental document of the Quebec legislative framework for transparency and participation in public policy development. While an analysis of the entire legal framework for facilitating public participation is not the subject of this report, concrete measures for achieving this objective that could be included in the Act are proposed throughout the analysis.

The Quebec legislator could conduct a reflection on the terminology used to qualify lobbying activities

In its Statement of Principles, The Quebec Commissioner of Lobbying uses the term "interest representative" instead of "lobbyist" to better reflect the nature of the activities of all individuals covered by this expression (Table 1.3), without, however, making any recommendations to the Quebec legislator on the use of this terminology.

Table 1.3. Terminology proposed by the Quebec Commissioner of Lobbying in its Statement of Principles

Definition	Lobbying Transparency and Ethics Act	Statement of Principles of the Quebec Commissioner of Lobbying
Any person, whether or not a salaried employee, whose occupation or mandate consists, in whole or in part, in lobbying on behalf of another person in return for compensation	Consultant lobbyist	External interest representative
Any person a significant part of whose job or function within a profit-seeking enterprise consists in lobbying on behalf of the enterprise	Enterprise lobbyist	Internal interest representative
Any person a significant part of whose job or function consists in lobbying on behalf of an association or other non-profit group	Organisation lobbyist	

Source: (Lobbyisme Québec, 2019[8]).

The Quebec Commissioner of Lobbying points out that the terms "lobbying" and "lobbyist" have little resonance in a large part of public opinion, and are sometimes spontaneously associated with hidden or even illegal activities, fuelling the perception of collusion between corporate interests and public officials. The context in which the Act was adopted, following a political scandal revealing privileged links between a public relations firm and the government in 2002, may have contributed to the feeling that only certain activities should be associated with the word "lobbying" and be subject to legislative measures aimed at preventing certain abuses. Lobbying is often discussed in the public debate to highlight the lack of transparency in the dialogue between certain large industries and public decision-makers.

As a result, the practical reality of lobbying is rarely discussed. Various surveys conducted for the Quebec Commissioner of Lobbying in 2018 revealed that a majority of citizens consider that lobbying activities carried out with public institutions are not legitimate, while one elected official or public servant out of four questioned the very legitimacy of lobbying (Lobbyisme Québec, 2019[8]). During various consultations conducted by the Quebec Commissioner of Lobbying, some parliamentary and municipal elected officials pointed out that the terminology of the Act also contributed to its misunderstanding and to the public's mistrust.

This negative connotation is also found in other OECD countries, where the term is still misunderstood and even used to call for the exclusion of certain interests from any public policy discussion, which may be against the basic principles of democratic participation. Moreover, these negative perceptions of lobbying have led to the emergence in the public debate of other terms that are perceived more positively, such as advocacy.

In Quebec, the OECD's interviews with non-profit organisations (NPO) not subject to the Act confirmed that these organisations refuse to see their activities associated with the term "lobbying", and consider that this term only covers activities with profit-making objectives. The use of these conceptual demarcations - "business-lobbying" and "NPO-advocacy" - does, however, reflect a common purpose of these activities, namely to convince public decision-makers and influence the processes of developing and implementing public policy (Darut and Germond, 2021[15]). Some of the stakeholders interviewed also agreed that their influencing activities were akin to representation activities with public authorities.

In this context, the Quebec legislator could conduct a reflection on the terminology used to qualify lobbying activities in the legal framework. The need for this reflection is fully in line with Principle 2 of the OECD Recommendation, which emphasises that jurisdictions should weigh all available regulatory and policy options to select an appropriate solution that addresses key concerns such as accessibility and integrity, and takes into account the national context, for example the level of public trust and measures necessary to achieve compliance. (Principle 2 of the Recommendation).

Several OECD countries have chosen to integrate all these categorisations into a single term "interest representative". Germany, for example, without abandoning the terminology of "lobbying" in the wording of the law and the name of the register ("Lobbyregister"), nevertheless uses the term "interest representation" in its definitions of "lobbying" and "lobbyist" (Table 1.4).

Table 1.4. Alternative terminologies used in international lobbying legislations

	Law / regulation	Categories of lobbyists	Definition
Germany	Act on the Establishment of a Lobbying Register for the Representation of Special Interests in the German Bundestag and the Federal Government (Lobbying Register Act - Lobbyregistergesetz)	Representatives of special interests	**Representatives of special interests** are all natural or legal persons, partnerships or other organisations, including those in the form of networks, platforms or other forms of collective activities which engage in the representation of special interests themselves or commission such representation on their behalf.
Austria	Federal Law No. 64/2012 on the Transparency of Lobbying and Advocacy Activities	• Lobbying firms • Companies employing company lobbyists • Self-governing bodies • Advocacy groups	**Lobbying firms**: companies whose business purpose is to carry out lobbying activities for clients in return for payment; **Companies employing company lobbyists**: companies employing staff for the purpose of lobbying on their own behalf on condition that a significant amount of his/her responsibilities is taken up by lobbying activities; **Self-governing bodies**: bodies established by law to represent the professional or common interests of its members. This includes the Chamber of Commerce and Labour and professional associations; **Advocacy groups**: legal associations of private individuals.
France	Law n° 2013-907 of 11 October 2013 on transparency in public life (Section 3 bis: Transparency of relations between interest representatives and public authorities)	Interest representatives	**Interest representatives - organisations"**: directors, employees or members of legal persons under private law who communicate with public officials with the aim of influencing public decisions. **"Interest representatives – self-employed individuals"**: natural persons who are not employed by a legal person who initiate communications with public officials with the aim of influencing public decisions.
Peru	Law 28024 regulating the management of interests in the public administration	Person who performs an act of interest management	**"Person who performs an interest management act"**: natural or legal person, national or foreign, who conducts interest management actions on behalf of their own interests or the interests of third parties, in relation to public decisions to be adopted by officials with public decision-making capacity.
Slovenia	Integrity and Prevention of Corruption Act of 2010	Interest groups	**"Interest groups"** means legal persons governed by private law, and other legally regulated forms of association of natural or legal persons, on behalf and for the account of which a lobbyist performs a lobbying activity.
Spain	Code of Conduct for Members of Congress and the Senate	Interest groups	**Interest groups** are natural or legal persons, or entities without legal personality, that communicates directly or indirectly with holders of public or elected office or their personnel in favour of private, public, or collective interests, seeking to modify or influence issues related to the drafting or modification of legislative initiatives.
European Union	Interinstitutional Agreement of 20 May 2021 between the European Parliament, the Council of the European Union and the European Commission on a mandatory transparency register	Interest representative	Any natural or legal person, or formal or informal group, association or network, that engages in covered activities

Source: (OECD, 2021[1]).

However, these considerations will have to be carefully considered by the Quebec legislator and weighed against their expected impact on perceptions of lobbying in Quebec, and on the consistency of the legal framework with that of other Canadian jurisdictions if such a change in terminology were to be proposed by the legislator. Indeed, the laws in force at the federal level and in Canadian jurisdictions all use the terminology of "lobbying" and "lobbyist", allowing for a consistent approach to transparency across all levels of government.

At a minimum, Quebec could align the terminology of the Act with the categories identified in the laws in force at the federal level and in Canadian jurisdictions. Indeed, these jurisdictions do not distinguish in their definitions between enterprise lobbyists and organisation lobbyists into two distinct categories, but group all individuals who lobby on behalf of their employer into a single category - "in-house lobbyist" - which includes both commercial and non-profit organisations, although different obligations apply depending on the nature of these organisations.

Given the specific context of Quebec, it will be up to the legislator to judge the best way to understand the legal terminology qualifying lobbying activities, so as to change the public's perception and foster confidence in the public policy-making process.

Adapting the scope of the law to the different local levels and taking into account existing regulatory frameworks

The OECD Recommendation on Principles for Transparency and Integrity in Lobbying stresses that jurisdictions should not directly replicate rules and guidelines from one jurisdiction to another, but instead assess the potential and limitations of various policy and regulatory options and apply the lessons learned in other systems to their own context. In particular, the scale and nature of the lobbying industry within their jurisdictions is a key factor to be taken into account (Principle 2 of the Recommendation). Furthermore, rules and guidelines on lobbying should be consistent with the wider policy and regulatory frameworks (Principle 3 of the Recommendation), including regulatory frameworks already in place can support a culture of transparency and integrity in lobbying, and the scope of application should be sufficiently explicit to avoid misinterpretation and to prevent loopholes. (Principle 4 of the Recommendation). In this perspective, it is appropriate to:

- Address the governance concerns raised by lobbying practices at all stages of the legislative, regulatory, policy or administrative policy cycle.
- Consider a greater adaptation of the scope of application for certain individualised decisions without general or normative scope, depending on the local level or the public decision concerned.
- Take into account broader policy and regulatory arrangements implemented since the adoption of the Act in 2002.
- Ensure that all risk sectors are covered by the scope.
- Precisely define and clarify the public decision-makers covered in order to avoid any confusion in the application of the Act.

The scope of public decisions covered could include all stages of the legislative, regulatory, policy or administrative policy cycle

In Quebec, the Act covers any oral or written communication with a public office holder in an attempt to influence or that may reasonably be considered by the initiator of the communication as capable of influencing a decision concerning:

- The development, introduction, amendment or defeat of any legislative or regulatory proposal, resolution, policy, program or action plan.

- The issue of any permit, licence, certificate or other authorisation.
- The awarding of any contract, otherwise than by way of a call for public tenders, or of any grant or other financial benefit or the granting of any other form of benefit determined by government regulation, or
- The appointment of certain public office holders (Article 3 of the Act).

In its Statement of principles, the Quebec Commissioner of Lobbying considers that lobbying activities with respect to policy should be subject to a comprehensive regime and that their disclosure is considered relevant to inform the public. The organisation proposes to define as a lobbying activity relevant to the public and to require the disclosure of any intervention, either direct or through an intermediary, with a public institution, whose goal is:

- To suggest or change the development, content, drafting or implementation of any type of legislative, regulatory, strategic or administrative policy; or
- To influence the appointment of any person holding a key position within the State; or
- To influence the decision-making process of a public institution concerning any financial investment, contract, permit or other authorisation determined by the Act or by regulation (Principle 1 of the Statement of Principles).

With respect to the development, content, formulation or implementation of any form of legislative, regulatory, policy or administrative direction, the Quebec Commissioner of Lobbying's proposal is in line with the OECD Recommendation, which stresses that rules and guidelines on lobbying should address the governance concerns related to lobbying practices (Principle 2 of the Recommendation), and that they should be sufficiently unambiguous so as not to be open to misinterpretation and to avoid regulatory loopholes (Principle 4 of the Recommendation). Indeed, influence may occur in the setting of a policy agenda, in the development and adoption of policies; some decisions may also be influenced in the implementation or evaluation phases (Figure 1.2 and Table 1.5).

Figure 1.2. The policy-making process

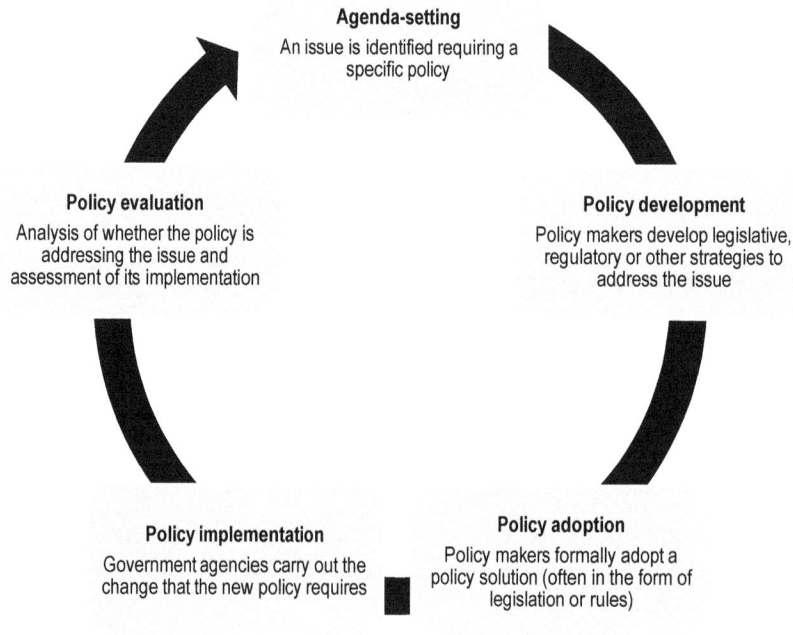

Source: (OECD, 2017[2]).

Table 1.5. Risks of undue influence along the policy cycle

		Agenda-setting	Policy development	Policy adoption	Policy implementation	Policy evaluation
Risk of undue influence on...		Priorities	Draft laws and regulations, policy documents (e.g. project feasibility studies, project specifications)	Votes (laws) or administrative decisions (regulations), changes to draft laws or project specifications	Implementation rules and procedures	Evaluation results
Main actors targeted	Legislative level	Legislators, ministerial staff, political parties	Legislators, ministerial Staff, political parties	Legislators, parliamentary commissions and committees, invited experts	-	Parliamentary commissions and committees, invited experts
	Administrative level	Civil servants, technical experts, consultants	Civil servants, technical experts, consultants	Heads of administrative bodies or units	Civil servants	Civil servants, consultants (experts)

Source: (OECD, 2017[2]).

The rules and guidelines for transparency and integrity in lobbying are not intended to cover all the risks specified above. Rather, they are part of a framework of policies and regulations that contribute to a culture of transparency and integrity in public policy-making and implementation processes. This includes stakeholder engagement through public consultation and participation, the right to petition government, freedom of information legislation, rules on political parties and election campaign financing, codes of conduct for public officials and lobbyists, mechanisms for keeping regulatory and supervisory authorities accountable and effective provisions against illicit influencing (Principle 3 of the Recommendation).

However, the Quebec Commissioner of Lobbying's proposal could be clarified to include any intervention, directly or through an intermediary, with a public institution for the purpose of :

- Suggesting the development of any form of legislative, regulatory, policy or administrative direction, and making proposals regarding its content, formulation and implementation (i.e. seek the adoption of a public decision).
- Changing the development, content and wording of any form of legislative, regulatory, policy or administrative direction being planned (i.e. influence a public decision that has not yet been adopted).
- Changing the content, formulation, implementation and evaluation of any form of legislative, regulatory or administrative policy in force, or request its removal (i.e. influence, to obtain its modification or removal, a public decision in force).

Covering the appointment of any person to a key position within the State is good international practice and should be included in the Act. Indeed, decisions on the appointment of certain public officials can be a key area of interest for lobbyists, allowing them to advance their interests if a person in line with their specific interests is placed in the position concerned. In France and the United States, the appointment of certain public officials is considered a type of decision covered by lobbying activities and is therefore covered by transparency requirements (Box 1.3).

> **Box 1.3. Individual appointment decisions are covered in France and the US**
>
> **France**
>
> The decisions covered by lobbying activities were specified in Law 2016/1691 for the promotion of transparency, combating corruption and the modernisation of the economy (Article 25). Under the heading of "other public decisions", the contours of which are not specified, the High Authority for the Transparency of Public Life considers that these cover "individual appointment decisions".
>
> **United States**
>
> The decisions covered by lobbying activities are specified in the Lobbying Disclosure Act (section 3 "Definitions"). They include appointments or confirmations of a person to a position subject to confirmation by the Senate.
>
> Source: (OECD, 2021[1]).

Decisions concerning financial contributions, contracts, permits or other authorisations are addressed in the next two sections.

The Act could allow for a greater adaptation of the disclosure of lobbying activities for certain public decisions without general scope and according to the institutional levels concerned

Quebec's Lobbying Act covers a broad spectrum of public decisions and institutions, and remains one of the most comprehensive and encompassing among OECD jurisdictions. At the time of its adoption in 2002, the Act covered parliamentary, government and municipal public institutions. Thus, the same legal and institutional framework applies to lobbying activities targeting the Quebec government as it does to activities carried out at the municipal level. Other cases exist in countries where the same institutional framework covers several levels of government (Figure 1.3 and Box 1.4).

Figure 1.3. Lobbying regulations targeting local governments in OECD countries

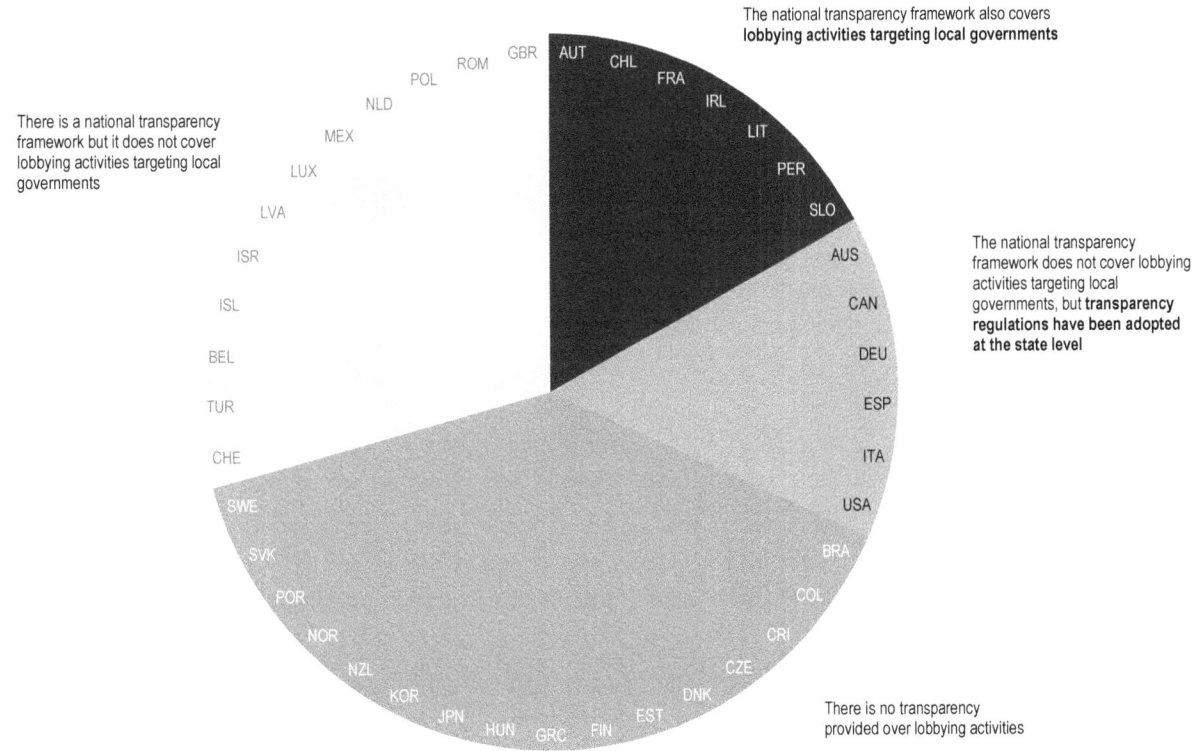

Source: (OECD, 2021[1]).

> **Box 1.4. The national transparency framework also covers lobbying of local governments**
>
> In **Austria**, the Federal Act No. 64/2012 on the transparency of lobbying and advocacy activities covers activities targeting provincial governors, provincial legislators, mayors and members of their cabinets.
>
> In **Chile**, Law No. 20/730 regulating lobbying and representation of private interests to authorities and public officials covers activities targeting regional directors of public services, governors, regional ministerial secretaries, regional councillors, mayors, executive secretaries of regional councils, as well as municipal secretaries.
>
> In **France**, the Law n° 2013-907 of 11 October 2013 on the transparency of public life will cover the local level from 1 July 2022, including presidents of regions, mayors of cities with more than 150,000 inhabitants. This broad definition will make the register one of the largest in the world, eventually covering 19,000 public officials.
>
> In **Ireland**, "designated public officers" (DPOs) under the Lobbying Act 2015 cover several positions in local authorities (chief executives, deputy chief executives, directors of services, finance officers, human resources officers).
>
> In **Lithuania**, the "persons subject to lobbying activities" specified in the Law No. VIII-1749 on Lobbying Activities include mayors, members of municipal councils, directors of municipal administrations and their deputies.
>
> Finally, in **Slovenia**, the Integrity and Corruption Prevention Act of 2010 covers activities targeting civil servants and public officials employed in local governments.
>
> Source: (OECD, 2021[1]).

However, in OECD jurisdictions, Quebec remains one of the only frameworks applied at the provincial level that also applies at the municipal level. Indeed, in countries with a national or federal transparency framework that does not cover local government lobbying, transparency regulations have generally been adopted at the state level, but these do not usually cover the municipal level as a whole. In these states or provinces, separate regulations exist at the municipal level (Box 1.5).

> **Box 1.5. The national transparency framework does not cover lobbying activities targeting local governments, but regulations have been adopted at state and municipal level**
>
> **Australia**
>
> Several states (Western Australia, New South Wales, Queensland, South Australia, Tasmania, Victoria, Australian Capital Territory) have adopted lobbying codes and registers, with similar registration requirements for consultant lobbyists lobbying in those states.
>
> **Canada**
>
> Except for Northwest Territories and Nunavut, all provinces and territories of Canada have adopted a specific framework regulating the interactions between public officials and lobbyists. These regulations usually include similar definitions and transparency requirements as the regulation at the federal level.
>
> In particular, the lobbying regime in Québec regulates lobbying activities at governmental, parliamentary and municipal levels, ensuring consistency in the application of the regime throughout the Québec jurisdiction and its public institutions. In Newfoundland and Labrador, the regulation also applies to the City of St. John's Municipal Council and its controlled entities.
>
> In other Canadian jurisdictions, lobbying activities have also been regulated at the municipal level. The City of Ottawa introduced a 2012 Lobbyist Code of Conduct and a Lobbyist Registry. The City's Integrity Commissioner oversees the implementation of the Lobbyist Registry and the enforcement of the Code of Conduct. Similarly, the Lobbyist Registrar of the City of Toronto maintains an online municipal registry of lobbyists and lobbying activities, established in 2018 by a lobbying by-law modifying the Toronto Municipal Code. The Lobbyist Registrar is one of the City's four Accountability Officers, and oversees compliance with the Code of Conduct for lobbyists independently.
>
> Other regulations exist in the municipalities of Brampton, Hamilton, Vaughan and Winnipeg, for example.
>
> **Spain**
>
> In Spain, several states (Aragon, Castilla-La Mancha, Catalonia, Valencia, Navarra) have adopted regulations on lobbying. The city of Madrid also adopted its own regulation in 2017.
>
> **United States**
>
> All states have adopted their own lobbying regulations. Some of these laws cover part of the municipal level, such as New York State, where the regulation applies to any municipality with a population of over 5 000. Specific regulations also exist at the municipal level, such as in New York, Chicago, Los Angeles, San Diego, San Francisco, Austin and San Jose.
>
> Source: (OECD, 2021[1]), (Sunlight Foundation, 2013[16]), (National Conference of State Legislatures, 2021[17]).

The Quebec regime ensures that public decision-makers, lobbyists and Quebec citizens, regardless of where they reside in Quebec, have access to the same legal framework, which reinforces its coherence, makes it easier to understand and avoids a multiplication of divergent frameworks at different local levels. In this respect, the Quebec Act is one of the most comprehensive and coherent among OECD countries, and it is therefore desirable to maintain the coverage of the current Act with respect to municipalities. However, an undifferentiated application of the Act to all levels of government and to all public decisions without taking into account the reality of municipalities may undermine the objective of transparency of the Act and its effective implementation. The Quebec regime, which has no equivalent in international jurisdictions, must take into account the specificities of local public life, which increases the complexity of the application of the regime. The challenges to be taken into account include:

- **The density and continuity of relations between local actors and public officials, which is higher in municipal settings.** Many citizens' associations, community groups, sports clubs, local residents' or young entrepreneurs' groups, as well as small and medium-sized enterprises, are active at the municipal level. These groups are generally less structured than the interest groups represented at the provincial level and have fewer resources. Above all, they seek a close relationship with local elected officials and are in regular contact with elected officials and civil servants in the municipalities. Reporting requirements for these actors for too many administrative decisions could be disproportionate if they are not adapted to different levels of government.

- **The heterogeneity of the local and municipal environment.** The municipal organisation in Quebec is characterised by a limited number of municipalities with significant human and financial resources on the one hand, and a wide range of medium and small municipalities with more or less significant resources on the other. In addition, there are supra-municipal structures such as the regional county municipalities (RCMs). When it comes to managing the application of the Act, the reality of large cities can therefore differ considerably from that of small municipalities. As a result, limited financial and human resources, as well as weaker capacities, may weaken public management and control, and call for a simplified regime for the regulation of lobbying activities.

- **The close links between some corporate interests and local political elites.** These links can lead to clientelistic practices and concentration of power, which undermines accountability and equity of access to public officials.

Taking these specificities into account requires finding compromises between the objective of transparency of the law, the risks in local public management and the requirements for the proper functioning of local democracy, for example the need to maintain a citizen dialogue with public institutions.

In its Diagnostic, the Quebec Commissioner of Lobbying deplores the fact that the scope of public decisions covered by lobbying activities is not distinguished according to the public institutions involved, whether municipal or provincial, the type of contract or the amount of funding. This absence of modulation according to the various institutional levels leads to a lesser readability of the information declared on the register, and runs the risk of diluting control and verification activities. In its Statement of Principles, the Commissioner of Lobbying proposes to establish, by regulation, specific, adapted rules concerning the regulation and disclosure of certain lobbying activities towards different levels of public institutions, especially concerning any form of financial investment, contract, permit or other form of authorisation that it is relevant to regulate (Principle 3 of the Statement of Principles).

The Commissioner of Lobbying considers that the legislative framework should cover all decisions concerning legislative, regulatory or strategic orientations, regardless of the institutional level. However, the Statement of Principles considers that lobbying activities should be disclosed when they relate to decisions concerning the granting of contracts, permits, authorisations or financial contributions in a manner that is adapted to the nature of these activities, their context and the institutions involved. Taking into account the specificity of the Quebec regime, which applies to both the provincial and municipal levels, as well as the exclusions already provided for in the Act (Box 1.6), it seems necessary to adapt the categories of decisions that would be considered relevant at different institutional levels and thus provide that the obligation to declare is only imposed on certain local public decisions.

> **Box 1.6. Exclusions under the Lobbying Transparency and Ethics Act (Section 5)**
>
> - Communications for the sole purpose of inquiring as to the nature or scope of the legal rights or obligations of a client, an enterprise or a group.
> - Any submission made by a person other than a consultant lobbyist concerning the granting of a permit, licence, certificate, authorisation, subsidy or pecuniary benefit, where the public office holder having the power to make the decision is only authorised in this regard to ascertain whether the legal requirements for the granting of such benefit are satisfied. The provision of documents or information required by a public office holder for the processing of that request is also excluded.
> - Any submission made in response to a written request from a public office holder, including any submission made in response to a call for public tenders issued under the public office holder's authority.
> - Any submission made in the negotiation of an individual or collective labour contract or in the negotiation of a collective agreement for the provision of professional services.
> - Any submission for the sole purpose of informing a public office holder of the existence and characteristics of a product or service (outside the contractual process).
> - Communications for the sole purpose of enquiring about the process of obtaining a contract or about the requirements for the acquisition of goods.
> - Communications for the sole purpose of obtaining information about a product that an organisation wishes to acquire.
> - Communications within the framework of a call for tenders (such as the submission of the tender and the required documents or a simple request for information sent to the representative of the organisation designated in the call for tenders within the deadline for submitting a tender).
> - Any submission made in the negotiation, subsequent to the awarding of a contract, of conditions for the performance of the contract. However, the Act applies to discussions concerning significant changes to the contract or its renewal.
>
> Source: (Légis Québec, 2002[7])

Several approaches can thus be taken. First, some of the exclusions in Article 5 of the Act concerning individualised decisions could be clarified and broadened. For example, the granting of funding, the allocation of which is a right for those who meet the legal requirements for obtaining it, could be excluded from the scope of the Act, regardless of the local level. In France, for example, the granting of an authorisation or the receipt of a benefit, the granting of which constitutes a right for those who fulfil the legal conditions for obtaining it, is not covered by the lobbying framework (Box 1.7). Communications made with a view to obtaining a grant awarded in accordance with the government policy "*L'action communautaire: une contribution essentielle à l'exercice de la citoyenneté et au développement social du Québec*" (Community Action: A crucial contribution to the exercise of citizenship and social development in Québec) could therefore be excluded from the registration requirement (Gouvernement du Québec, 2001[18]).

> **Box 1.7. In France, the granting of an authorisation or the benefit of an advantage, the granting of which constitutes a right for persons who fulfil the legal conditions for obtaining it, is not covered by the lobbying framework**
>
> In France, individual decisions aimed at issuing, modifying, withdrawing or renewing an approval, authorisation, certification, derogation, dispensation, exemption, accreditation, registration on a list, licence, permit, title, or financial benefit of any kind are included in the scope of the Act.
>
> However, Article 1 of the Decree of 9 May 2017 nevertheless provides for an exception to this principle, specifying that "the fact of requesting, in application of legislative or regulatory provisions, the issue of an authorisation or a financial benefit of any kind does not constitute a communication within the meaning of the preceding paragraph, the delivery of an authorisation or the benefit of an advantage, the granting of which constitutes a right for persons who meet the legal conditions for obtaining it, as well as the fact of submitting an administrative appeal or taking a step which, by virtue of the applicable law, is necessary for the delivery of an authorisation, the exercise of a right or the granting of an advantage."
>
> By extension, the High Authority for the transparency of public life considers more generally that not all exchanges of information that take place between a legal person and a public official in the context of following up a request for an individual decision, whatever it may be, constitute communications. These exchanges are not intended to influence the individual decision in question, and therefore cannot be considered as interest representation. This exclusion is specifically aimed at the following situations:
>
> - Prior to the submission of an application, communications with the competent authority that are limited to announcing the submission, specifying the nature and characteristics of the operation or agreeing on a timetable.
> - During the appraisal of the application, all communications between the applicant and the administration competent to process it. This exclusion applies only to communications between the applicant and the competent administration concerning the decision in question during the appraisal period.
> - In the event of refusal of the application, communications which take place in the context of an informal, hierarchical or contentious appeal.
> - In case of acceptance of the request, all communications that are limited to the follow-up of the implementation of the individual decision.
>
> Source: (HATVP, 2021[19]).

Secondly, the Act could adopt a risk-based approach and consider only the most sensitive decisions in terms of the specific reality of a given territory or organisation. For example, communications relating to individualised decisions (grants, permits, licences, certificates or other authorisations) could be excluded in small municipalities in favour of decisions of general application (standards, guidelines, programmes and action plans). In a less restrictive approach, consideration could be given to establishing thresholds for financial contributions, permits or other authorisations granted by a municipal body, such as representations made as part of an administrative process established under a defined programme for obtaining a grant, financial assistance, loan, loan guarantee or bond in an amount below a pre-determined threshold. Such thresholds are, for example, applied for certain financial contributions in the cities of New York or Austin. Decisions on public procurement are discussed in the section below.

The Act could take into account the advances in transparency and integrity allowed by the Act respecting contracting by public bodies

Ensuring integrity, effectiveness and efficiency in public procurement depends on fair access to procurement opportunities by potential competitors of all sizes, but also on an adequate degree of transparency in contract management. This is a fundamental principle of the OECD Recommendation on Public Procurement and the OECD Recommendation on Public Integrity (OECD, 2015[20]; OECD, 2017[21]). Indeed, disclosure of information at all stages of the contract management cycle helps to identify and subsequently mitigate mismanagement, fraud and corruption, and to increase the accountability of clients. Transparency also ensures the fair and equitable treatment of potential suppliers, while allowing important and relevant information to be easily accessible to all stakeholders.

The Government of Quebec has made significant progress in recent years towards establishing an institutional framework of integrity in public procurement processes applicable to public and municipal organisations and reducing undue influence by businesses in the conduct of public procurement (OECD, 2020[22]). Thus, two distinct institutional frameworks apply in the Quebec public sector: one governing contracts of government ministries and agencies (public bodies) and the other governing contracts of municipal bodies (Table 1.6).

Table 1.6. Regulatory framework for awarding public contracts in Quebec

Regulatory frameworks	Lead Ministry	Targeted networks	Number
Public bodies	Treasury Board Secretariat (RBS)	Ministries and agencies Education Network Health and Social Services Network State-owned enterprises	350
Municipal bodies	Ministry of Municipal Affairs and Housing (MAMH)	Municipalities Municipal bodies	+/- 1 500

Source: (OECD, 2020[22]).

As in the contract management systems of OECD countries and elsewhere, there are three types of procedures in Quebec: "the call for tenders (CFT)", which is the general procedure used, "the invitation to tender", ITT and direct award contracts (DCA). In Quebec, different CFT thresholds can be applied because public and municipal bodies are subject to different procurement liberalisation agreements. The thresholds therefore vary according to the status of the different bodies and whether or not the contracts are for supplies, services, information technology, or construction work. In certain situations, a direct agreement contract can be concluded when the amount of the contract is higher than the thresholds for public tendering. These include emergency situations, situations where only one contractor is possible, where the contract involves a matter of a confidential or protected nature, and where tendering would not be in the public interest.

Below the CFT thresholds, Quebec's regulatory framework ensures sound contract management by imposing a number of mechanisms on public bodies, including the possibility of:

- Proceeding by CFT or ITT.
- Competitor rotation.
- Putting in place control provisions related to the total value of the contract and any additional expenditure.
- Establishing a monitoring mechanism to ensure the effectiveness and efficiency of the procedures used.

- Introducing, subject to any applicable cross-governmental agreement, measures promoting the procurement of goods, services, or construction works from competitors or contractors in the region concerned.

Accordingly, each public entity has internal regulations indicating the procedures to be followed in accordance with its principles. Municipalities are also required to adopt a contract management regulation, make it available on the internet and transmit it to the Ministry. They are able to put in place any rules they wish for the award of contracts involving expenditure of less than USD 100 000 as long as they adopt regulations on contract management specifying the circumstances in which these different modes will apply.

The establishment of the Autorité des marchés publics (AMP), with its audit and oversight powers, further strengthens the integrity framework for public contracts. Its monitoring mandate, as well as its powers of order for public bodies and of recommendation for municipal bodies, play a key role in strengthening integrity in the conduct of all public contracts in Quebec.

To increase transparency, Quebec has the Electronic Tendering System (SEAO). In terms of functionality, the SEAO is used mainly as a platform for publishing notices and documents relating to public contracts. Indeed, the publication of CFT documents on the SEAO is mandatory for all public bodies. The results of CFTs must also be published on the SEAO when this procedure is used. One of the aims of this measure was to combat collusion and malpractice in public procurement more effectively by avoiding direct contacts between potential bidders, as well as between potential bidders and public procurement officials. Since the introduction of this requirement, public and municipal bodies no longer communicate directly with bidders before the result of the tender is determined. The purpose of this practice is not to give a company an advantage over its competitors by providing it with privileged information.

In particular, the Quebec government has implemented targeted communications to make bidders aware of its ethical and lobbying standards. The Government of Québec requires public works contractors (PWCs) to include a questionnaire in their call for tenders to find out why a company did not submit a bid, even though it obtained the tender documents. In addition, the call for tenders documents recall the rules to be followed under the *Lobbying Transparency and Ethics Act* and the *Code of Conduct for Lobbyists*. Each bidder must attach to its bid a declaration stating that the communications, if any, were made in accordance with the Act and the Code. However, the OECD had made a number of recommendations to enhance transparency in the conduct of public procurement, including the publication of meetings with suppliers.

In order to avoid duplicating or overlapping the disclosure of information, the Quebec Commissioner of Lobbying proposes to take into account the transparency and ethics processes already in place and adopted since the Act came into force, particularly with respect to the awarding of public contracts (Principle 1 of the Statement of Principles). In particular, the Commissioner is of the opinion that the lobbying regime should not seek to compensate for the shortcomings of other transparency and disclosure regimes put in place by the State and for which the relevance of the information has already been considered, especially since exclusions are already provided for in the Act (Box 1.6).

Currently, the Act covers the award of a contract other than through a public tender. Influential communications made upstream to define needs and technical specifications are therefore covered, while communications that take place after the CFT has been launched are excluded.

In light of the above, it seems justified to better delimit by law or by regulation the decision-making processes of a public institution concerning any contract covered by a lobbying framework. This could involve, for example, excluding from the scope of the Act the awarding of some or all (below a certain value threshold) DCA concluded at the municipal level insofar as each public entity has internal regulations or contract management regulations governing the awarding of this type of contract.

However, it seems essential to cover the needs definition and procurement planning stage, which is particularly vulnerable to undue influence and corruption in large infrastructure projects, notably because of the degree of government discretion over investment decisions, the size of the sums involved, the technical complexity of the projects and the multiple stages of the investment cycle (OECD, 2017[23]). The influence of political interests, particularly at the stages of defining investment needs and programming projects, can lead to waste and the creation of 'white elephants' (i.e. infrastructure that does not meet needs and whose costs are not justified by its utility). In France, for example, the needs definition stage is covered by the lobbying regime, and some communications are then excluded once the call for tender has been completed, as is currently the case in Quebec (Box 1.8). This would be covered by Principle 1 of the Statement of Principles and the previous recommendation to cover influence on policy or administrative directions.

Box 1.8. The definition of needs and competitive tendering procedures in France

In France, certain communications relating to competitive tendering procedures on the basis of Article 42 of Order No 2015-899 of 23 July 2015 on public contracts or Article 36 of Order No 2016-65 of 29 January 2016 on concession contracts are not covered by the framework regime.

Thus, the head of a company specialising in IT security, who approaches the office of the Minister of Defence to convince him of the need to launch a public procurement contract for the acquisition of data encryption technology with a view to reinforcing the security of the ministry's information systems, is carrying out an action of representation of interests. On the other hand, once the Ministry launches the competitive tendering procedure, its relations with this company and with the other candidates, until the contract is signed, are excluded from the scope of representation of interests, as are the relations that will be established with the selected candidate for the execution of the contract.

Source: (HATVP, 2021[19]).

To strengthen the coherence of the scope of application, the Act could also cover the Education network

The entry into force of the Act to modify the organisation and governance of the health and social services network, has extended the scope of application to health institutions (Table 1.1). Before 1 April 2015, only the Ministry of Health and health agencies were covered by the Act. The following institutions are now covered:

- Integrated Health and Social Services Centres (CISSS), Integrated University Health and Social Services Centres (CIUSSS).
- Non-merged institutions: Centre hospitalier de l'Université de Montréal; Centre hospitalier universitaire Sainte-Justine; McGill University Health Centre; Montreal Heart Institute; Institut Philippe-Pinel de Montréal; CHU de Québec - Université Laval; Institut universitaire de cardiologie et de pneumologie de Québec - Université Laval.
- Establishments that operate the following missions: local community service centre (CLSC), hospital centre (CH), residential and long-term care centre (CHSLD), child and youth protection centre or rehabilitation centre.

Public office holders in the health care system interviewed for this report confirmed the relevance of including this sector in the scope of application, given the risks involved in the acquisition of products or services in the hospital environment. Similar concerns exist in the education sector, which includes school boards, colleges and universities, and which is not covered by the legislative framework (with the exception of the *Ministère de l'Éducation et de l'Enseignement supérieur)*, even though it represents the second largest mission of the Quebec government in financial terms. The majority of elected officials and citizens consulted in 2018 as part of the establishment of the Diagnostic and the Statement of Principles of the Quebec Commissioner of Lobbying were in favour of making this public sector subject to the law.

Among Canadian jurisdictions, Prince Edward Island's regime covers lobbying of education departments, while New Brunswick's regime covers lobbying of the district education council and the board of directors of a regional health authority. Thus, to ensure consistency, the Quebec legislator could maintain the coverage of institutions in the health and social services network and consider including in the education network.

The law could cover all lobbying activities that are carried out with any elected official, officer or staff member of the public institutions covered by the scope

In order to ensure the effective enforcement of the Act, it is essential that all those engaged in lobbying activities be able to easily identify those who are considered public office holders within the meaning of the Act. In Quebec, the term "public office holder" refers to any elected official or person appointed to perform duties within the public administration:

- At the **parliamentary level**: the 125 Members of the National Assembly and their staff.
- At the **government level**: ministers, deputy ministers, cabinet staff and employees of the government and governmental organisations (approximately 350 ministries and agencies of the Quebec government).
- At the **municipal level:** mayors, municipal or borough councillors, wardens, chairs and other members of the council of a metropolitan community, as well as persons on their staff and employees of municipalities and municipal bodies (approximately 1 500 municipalities and municipal and supramunicipal organisations).

The Quebec Commissioner of Lobbying has pointed out on several occasions that since its adoption, the Act has been the source of many erroneous interpretations and questions from lobbyists and public office holders. In return for a greater precision in the scope of the public decisions covered, the Commissioner recommends that the provisions concerning public office holders be made easier to understand and that they "cover all public institutions and the elected officials, officers and employees of those institutions that lobbying activities may be directed towards, including the legislative, executive and administrative systems at the provincial and municipal levels" (Principle 6 of the Statement of principles). This principle implies that all provincial, municipal, educational and health care institutions are covered by the regime, without exception, as well as all elected officials, officers and staff of these institutions. The restrictions on the scope of application of the Act would thus not apply to the institutions or public officials covered, but to certain lobbying activities.

This provision is feasible and could facilitate the application and understanding of the Act to the extent that the previous recommendations come into force, in order to avoid an overly broad scope in the application of the Act and less relevance in the information reported. This approach has also been adopted in several OECD countries. In Australia, for example, all public officials of an organisation subject to transparency requirements are covered by the lobbying regime (Figure 1.4).

Figure 1.4. Ministers and Members of Parliament are usually covered by the requirements of lobbying regulations

Countries with a lobbying transparency framework

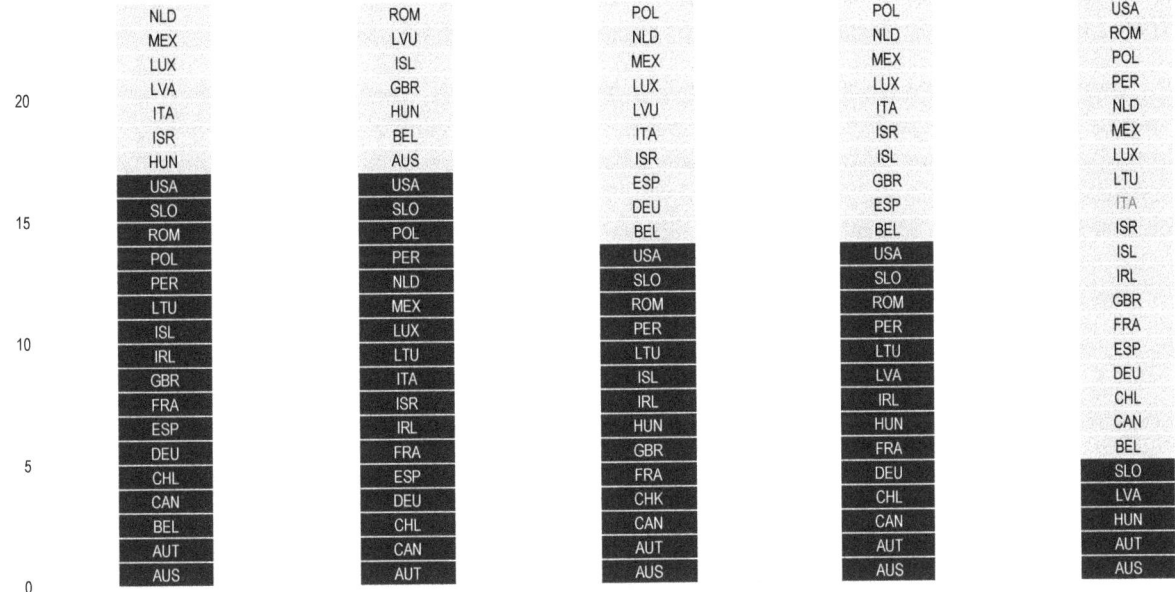

Source: Additional research by the OECD Secretariat.

However, it seems essential to implement a disclosure regime adapted to the category of public official targeted, so as not to burden the information requested in the register. In this case, a category of "designated public office holders" or "designated public officials", to whom specific disclosure obligations would apply and who should be listed in the register, could be maintained and specified either in the Act or in a regulation. This issue is discussed in more detail in Chapter 2.

Provide in the law a robust definition of the terms "lobbying" and "lobbyist" adapted to local realities and the changing lobbying landscape

To promote transparency and allow for public scrutiny, the OECD encourages countries to clearly define the terms 'lobbying' and 'lobbyist'" when they consider or develop rules and guidelines on lobbying. The definitions should be robust, comprehensive and sufficiently explicit to avoid misinterpretation and to prevent loopholes (Principle 4 of the Recommendation), while considering the administrative burden of compliance to ensure that it does not become an impediment to fair and equitable access to government (Principle 2 of the Recommendation). In this perspective, it is appropriate to:

- Consider the definition of 'lobbyist' in an inclusive way in order to ensure a level playing field for all interest groups, whether business or not-for-profit entities, which aim to influence public decisions.
- Provide for certain adaptations in order to strike a fair balance between the diversity of lobbying entities, their capacities and resources, with the measures to enhance transparency.
- Clearly specify the type of communications with public officials that are not considered 'lobbying' under the rules and guidelines.
- Clarify the thresholds above which activities are covered by the disclosure regime.

- Cover indirect lobbying activities, ensuring that the definition is adapted to changing practices and sufficiently unambiguous to avoid misinterpretation and regulatory loopholes.
- Include provisions on the participation of lobbyists in certain advisory groups.

The Act could make the activities of all interest groups engaged in lobbying transparent without making exceptions for different types of organisations

An adequate level of transparency on lobbying activities fosters transparency on who is influencing government policy or engaging in influential communications. This implies the clear identification of those actors who are considered lobbyists in the decision-making process. Non-profit organisations (NPOs) and associations of NPOs are subject to the Lobbying Transparency and Ethics Act. On the other hand, the Lobbying Transparency and Ethics Act Exclusions Regulation restricts the application of the Act to NPOs constituted for management, union or professional purposes or made up of a majority of for-profit enterprises or representatives of such enterprises (Table 1.7).

Table 1.7. Lobbyists subject to the Lobbying Transparency and Ethics Act

Consultant lobbyist	A consultant lobbyist is a person who engages in lobbying activities on behalf of others in return for compensation.
Enterprise lobbyist	The enterprise lobbyist is a person working for a profit-seeking enterprise, who carries out lobbying activities for a significant part on behalf of the enterprise.
Organisation lobbyist	The organisation lobbyist is a person for whom a significant part of their job or function consists in lobbying on behalf of a non-profit organisation (NPO) constituted to serve… • Management: Groups employers from a same sector, geographic area or sharing a common feature. For instance, the Association québécoise des centres de la petite enfance (AQCPE). • Union: Groups employees of a same sector or sharing a common feature. For example, the Confédération des syndicats nationaux (CSN). • Professional: A professional order constituted under the Professional Code or the Québec Interprofessional Council. For example, the Ordre des dentistes du Québec. OR Formed of members for which the majority are for-profit enterprises or representatives of such enterprises. For example, the Quebec Oil and Gas Association (QOGA) and the Association des libraires du Québec (ALQ)

Source: Lobbyisme Québec, https://lobbyisme.quebec/en/lobbyist/types-of-lobbyists/.

Thus, 20 years ago, the Quebec legislator chose to impose the obligation of transparency on certain types of actors whose activities involve the pursuit of a financial or corporate benefit, rather than delimiting a perimeter of actors subject to the obligation according to the nature of their communications of influence and their impact on public decision-making. Interest groups whose activities are aimed at promoting values or causes and not at pursuing financial or professional ends are not subject to registration. Under the current framework, not all actors conducting lobbying activities are therefore subject to transparency requirements. For example, lobbying aimed at influencing the content of a draft law should be registered if initiated by a company, whereas lobbying of the same nature to the same public decision-makers is currently not subject to any transparency measures if it is carried out by a non-profit organisation.

However, the OECD Recommendation, while stating that rules and guidelines should primarily target those who receive compensation for carrying out lobbying activities, such as consultant lobbyists and in-house lobbyists, also explicitly stresses that the definition of lobbying activities should also be considered more broadly and inclusively to provide a level playing field for interest groups, whether business or not-for-profit entities, which aim to influence public decisions (OECD, 2010[6]). Indeed, influence on public decision-making processes can be exercised by a wide range of actors and interest groups (Box 1.9). In addition, some non-profit organisations are increasingly resourced with financial means and a dedicated team to carry out lobbying activities.

> **Box 1.9. Influencing decision-making processes is not limited to direct communications between representatives of corporate interests and a public official**
>
> Influencing decision-making processes involves several types of actors, including:
>
> - **Companies** specialising in lobbying or public relations, law firms or independent lobbyists mandated to represent third party interests, such as companies or other organisations. These companies or individuals, usually located in key decision-making centres, have a deep understanding of the public policy-making process in a given jurisdiction. In countries with lobbying regulations, these actors are often referred to as "consultant lobbyists".
> - **Private companies** and their representatives through in-house lobbyists, or associations representing their interests (including sectoral or general associations such as chambers of commerce).
> - **Trade unions** and professional or industry associations representing employees or professions.
> - **Non-governmental organisations, charities, community organisations, foundations and religious organisations**. These organisations are the largest and most diverse group of actors influencing the public policy process. They bring causes to the attention of public policy makers, with a subjective view of the nature of the interests being defended. These organisations (be they public, corporate or state-funded) receive funding, usually from companies, public authorities or individuals, and represent specific interests and policy positions. They are increasingly numerous and organised (Colli and Adriaensen, 2018[24]).
> - **Research centres, think tanks and policy institutes**, which offer knowledge on specific problems and can propose solutions.
>
> Source: (OECD, 2021[1]).

Non-profit organisations are also active in changing existing law in order to translate the principles they advocate into law. Their activities are not limited to intervening in public fora, such as parliamentary committees or public consultations. They may engage in lobbying activities comparable to those of other actors when they seek to highlight the salient feature of a public policy issue, notably through research, awareness-raising and proposing amendments to the legislator (Darut and Germond, 2021[15]). NPOs interviewed by the OECD also confirmed that they conduct influence communications, such as written communications or meetings aimed at changing laws or policies, or the production of opinion pieces, research or publications that are sent to public office holders to defend a particular position. Increasing transparency on these activities is therefore also in the public interest. For example, an analysis of the origin of proposed amendments to legislation in France showed that non-governmental organisations have been particularly active in influencing legislative processes (Box 1.10).

> **Box 1.10. Origin of the sourced and proposed amendments on the anti-waste law in France**
>
> An analysis of the amendments proposed to the French deputies and senators in the framework of the "AGEC" bill (Law n° 2020-105 of 10 February 2020 on the fight against waste and the circular economy) showed that over 55% of the amendments came from non-governmental organisations, while 22% came from business federations. Of all the amendments sourced, thirteen amendments proposed by NGOs were adopted, and ten by business federations.
>
> However, the analysis focuses on amendments whose source is voluntarily disclosed by deputies and senators. This voluntary tracking may lead to an over-representation of NGOs and voluntary actors among the sourced amendments, as these may be perceived as more acceptable than those proposed by industry representatives, and therefore more disclosed by elected representatives.
>
> Source: (Communication & Institutions, 2020[25]).

This lack of accountability of NPOs may therefore be considered an obstacle to achieving the objectives of the Act with respect to transparency and the sound exercise of these activities. The regulatory regime for this type of influencing activity should not depend on the type of organisation represented, nor on its method of financing or its field of intervention. These criteria are not the most relevant when pursuing the objective of the law to make transparent influence communications targeting public office holders.

In its Statement of Principles, the Quebec Commissioner of Lobbying recommends regulating lobbying activities exercised by all interest representatives acting on behalf of an individual or entity, regardless of its nature, including a grouping of entities (Principle 4 of the Statement of Principles). This would align the regime in Quebec with most OECD jurisdictions that have established transparency mechanisms for lobbying practices (Table 1.8). In France, for example, all such groups, with the exception of religious organisations, are required to register in the register of interest representatives once they reach the registration threshold. Non-profit organisations are also covered in all Canadian provinces and at the federal level.

In other countries, such as Australia and the United Kingdom, these organisations are not automatically excluded from the scope of the law. Their coverage depends on the nature of their activities, not on their status or objectives. For example, in the United Kingdom, if one of these organisations communicates with ministers or permanent secretaries on behalf of paying clients, the activity must be disclosed. However, if they are communicating on their own behalf, the activity does not need to be registered.

Table 1.8. Actors subject to transparency requirements in their lobbying activities

OECD countries with transparency mechanisms in place for lobbying practices

	Consultant lobbyists (lobbying on behalf of third-party clients)	In-house lobbyists (companies or organisations)						
		Companies	NGOs /CSOs	Charities and foundations	Think tanks	Research centres	Religious organisations	Trade associations
Australia	●	○	○	○	○	○	○	○
Austria	●	●	●	●	●	●	○	●
Belgium	●	●	●	●	●	●	●	●
Canada	●	●	●	●	●	●	●	●
Chile	●	●	●	○	●	●	●	●
France	●	●	●	●	●	●	○	●
Germany	●	●	●	○	●	●	○	●
Iceland	●	●	●	●	●	●	●	●
Ireland	●	●	●	●	●	●	●	●
Israel	●	○	○	○	○	○	○	○
Italy	●	●	●	●	●	●	○	●
Lithuania	●	●	○	○	○	○	○	●
Mexico	●	●	●	●	●	●	●	●
Netherlands	●	●	●	●	●	●	●	●
Peru	●	●	●	●	●	●	●	●
Poland	●	○	○	○	○	○	○	○
Slovenia	●	●	●	●	●	●	●	●
Spain	●	●	●	●	●	●	●	●
United Kingdom	●	○	○	○	○	○	○	○
United States	●	●	●	●	●	●	○	●
European Union	●	●	●	●	●	●	●	●
● Yes	21	17	16	14	16	16	12	16
○ No	0	4	5	7	5	5	9	5

Source: (OECD, 2021[1]).

In these countries, as well as in Canadian jurisdictions, the general subjection of non-profit organisations to the rules and guidelines governing lobbying activities has not been as contested as in Quebec. These rules also provide for exclusions and exemptions applicable to NPOs. In Ireland, for example, the regular review of the implementation of the Lobbying Act of 2015 has revealed an overall acceptance of the regulatory regime, including by non-profit organisations that may have expressed concerns at the time the Act was introduced (Box 1.11). Specific exemptions and exclusions are discussed in the next section.

> **Box 1.11. Findings from two reviews of lobbying regulations in Ireland and Scotland**
>
> **Ireland**
>
> In Ireland, Section 2 of the Lobbying Act 2015 states that the Department of Public Expenditure and Reform must conduct regular reviews of the implementation of the Act. The first review of the Act took place in 2016 and the second in 2020.
>
> The consultations carried out for these reviews confirmed that overall the Act has been well received and implemented by the various stakeholders, and that the objective of transparency and accountability in lobbying has been achieved. Some of the non-profit organisations interviewed also stressed that their initial concerns expressed during debates on the Bill in 2012 about the potential inhibiting effects of the Act on their activities had been taken into account in the development of the framework. As a result, the Act has not been an obstacle to the continuation of their activities.
>
> **Scotland**
>
> In Scotland, a report commissioned by the Scottish Parliament on the implementation of the Lobbying Act 2016, confirmed that the Act did not have an inhibiting effect on the lobbying activities of not-for-profit organisations covered by the Act. Although the administrative burden has increased for these organisations, registration has also had benefits, such as increasing public awareness of the activities of these organisations to influence public policy on matters of public interest.
>
> Source: (Department of Public Expenditure and Reform, 2020[26]; Hepburn, 2017[27]).

However, the law could provide for some specific exemptions that take into account the diversity of non-profit organisations, their capacities and resources

The OECD Recommendation stresses that jurisdictions should take into account the scale and nature of their lobbying sector. Where the supply and demand for professional lobbying is limited, the Recommendation encourages jurisdictions to consider the effects of mandatory regulation to increase transparency, accountability and integrity in public life, and to take into account the administrative burden of compliance to ensure that it does not become an impediment to fair and equitable access to government.

In Quebec, for example, many small NPOs are composed solely or mainly of volunteers. The Quebec legislator and the Commissioner of Lobbying have already given careful thought to the issue of making non-profit organisations subject to the rules in Bill 56 (2016) which provided for all non-profit organisations to be subject to the rules (Box 1.12).

> **Box 1.12. Main provisions of the Bill 56 of 2015**
>
> The Bill made the following actors subject to the definition of an organisation lobbyist:
>
> - Employees, officers or board members of a non-profit organisation (including volunteers) who lobby for that organisation or for a non-profit organisation or unincorporated association of which that organisation is a member.
> - Individuals who hold office in an unincorporated group and who lobby for that group.
>
> Certain exemptions were provided, including influence communication activities carried out:
>
> - By volunteers of non-profit organisations.
> - By a natural person on behalf of an association composed solely of natural persons not incorporated as a non-profit organisation.
> - For a non-profit organisation by a volunteer who is not an employee, officer or board member of the organisation or who is not an employee, officer, board member, partner or shareholder of a for-profit business, related entity or member non-profit organisation.
> - In the case of an unincorporated association, by one of its volunteers who is not an employee, officer, board member, partner or shareholder of a for-profit business, related entity or non-profit organisation that is a member of that association.
> - For entering into an agreement or obtaining a grant to cover operating expenses or to support the overall mission of a non-profit organisation, in accordance with an existing law, regulation or programme.
> - To obtain a contract or financial assistance of USD 5 000 or less.
>
> Source: (Lobbyisme Québec, 2016[11]).

At the request of the National Assembly, the Commissioner of Lobbying conducted a study in June 2016 on subjecting all NPOs to the lobbying framework rules. This study, based on the consultation of representatives of 58 NPOs from various sectors of intervention and the reading of 64 briefs that had been submitted to the Commissioner, had the objective of identifying the difficulties faced by NPOs and proposing possible solutions to better implement the Act's transparency objective and citizens' right to information, while taking into account the specificities of collective action organisations (Table 1.9).

For example, there are approximately 8 000 organisations working in the field of community action in Quebec, of which 4 600 are supported by the Quebec government. These organisations are the result of citizens' initiatives and work to implement local services or activities based on the values of solidarity and democracy. When they are created, they are generally made up of volunteers and have recourse to philanthropic resources or support from municipalities or the Quebec government. There are also close to 350 groups of organisations supported by the Quebec government, which facilitate the work of community organisations and often provide representation, influence and mobilisation. The government policy on the recognition and support of community action, adopted by the Quebec government in 2001 and entitled "Community. Action: A crucial contribution to the exercise of citizenship and social development in Québec", as well as the Reference Framework for Community Action, already set out the relationship between community organisations and the State (Gouvernement du Québec, 2001[18]). According to this policy, "these organisations respond to the needs expressed by citizens who are experiencing a similar problematic situation or who share a common objective of well-being". As such, the Ministry of Labour, Employment and Social Solidarity (MESS), which is responsible for community action, works with three designated groups: the Réseau québécois de l'action communautaire autonome (RQ-ACA), the Réseau de l'action bénévole du Québec (RABQ) and the Réseau québécois de développement social (RQDS). Two other organisations also have this status of privileged interlocutor under the Social Economy Act: the Chantier de l'économie sociale and the Conseil québécois de la coopération et de la mutualité.

Table 1.9. Nomenclature of collective action organisations in Quebec

Category	Types of organisations	Main features
Community organisations (and groupings of organisations)	Community action organisations	Focused primarily on services to individuals and on meeting community service needs (e.g. sports or leisure clubs). They must meet the following criteria: • Have a non-profit status; • Demonstrate roots in the community; • Maintain a democratic and associative life; • Be free to determine their mission, orientations, approaches and practices.
	Autonomous community action organisations – Including collective advocacy organisations	Autonomous community action organisations are associated with the social movement of autonomous community action in which they participate (e.g. women's centres, collective advocacy organisations, community development corporations (CDCs), youth centres). In addition to meeting the four criteria listed above, they must meet the following criteria that reflect the nature of their actions in order to maintain distance from the state: • They must have been formed on the initiative of people in the community. • Pursue a social mission that is specific to the organisation and that promotes social transformation. • Demonstrate citizen practices and broad approaches based on the globality of the problem addressed. • Be directed by a board of directors that is independent of the public network. Collective advocacy organisations that have specific government recognition and are attached to a single ministry must meet the eight criteria for autonomous community action organisations, and have as their sole or primary mission: • Autonomous popular education activities focusing on rights and democratic life. • Social mobilisation activities. And also be active in any of the following categories of activities: • Advocacy activities. • Non-partisan political action activities.
Socio-economic action organisations	Philanthropic organisations	Promoting philanthropic activities (e.g. hospital and university foundations, family foundations, corporate foundations funded by private companies, service club foundations etc.)
	Socio-cultural organisations	Making social and cultural programming available to the community (e.g. festivals, symphony orchestras, theatres, museums, zoos, botanical gardens, aquariums, media, recreational and entertainment clubs and circles).
	Faith-based organisations	Promoting religious values and beliefs, performing religious services and rituals. These include auxiliary bodies (e.g. religious associations, Bible societies, congregations).
	Business and professional associations and trade unions	Support, govern and protect the interests of the business community (e.g. chambers of commerce, associations made up of a majority of for-profit businesses or representatives of such businesses), the labour community (e.g. central labour bodies) and the professional community (e.g. professional corporations, professional orders). These organisations are already subject to the Lobbying Transparency and Ethics Act.
	Student Associations	Associations or groups of student associations whose main functions are to represent pupils, students or student associations. Most of them are regulated by the Act on the Accreditation and Funding of Students' Associations.
	Political bodies	Promote partisan political action, such as political parties and their bodies; they must be authorised by the Chief Electoral Officer and are governed by the electoral laws.
	Advocacy organisations	Support, govern and protect the sole interests of their members, whether they are natural or legal persons (e.g. elite sports clubs, medical research centres, residents' groups, etc.).
	Economic development organisations	Organisations set up by a public authority to address economic development or business support interests.
	Social economy enterprises, cooperatives and mutuals	Produce and sell goods and services of various kinds (service organisations, such as credit unions). According to the Social Economy Act, "social economy" refers to all economic activities with a social purpose carried out by enterprises whose activities consist in particular in the sale or exchange of goods or services and which are operated in accordance with the following principles: • The purpose of the enterprise is to meet the needs of its members or the community.

Category	Types of organisations	Main features
		• The enterprise is not under the decision-making control of one or more public bodies (...).
		• The rules applicable to the enterprise provide for democratic governance by the members.
		• The enterprise aspires to economic viability.
		• The rules applicable to the enterprise prohibit the distribution of surpluses generated by its activities or provide for their distribution to members in proportion to the transactions carried out between each of them and the enterprise.
		• The rules applicable to the legal person operating the enterprise provide that in the event of dissolution, the remaining assets of the legal person must be vested in another legal person sharing similar objectives.

Source: (OECD, 2021[1]).

Some of the public office holders interviewed for this report also confirmed that these organisations can be seen as central partners of the state in certain areas, such as advocacy, health and social services, which places them in an atypical position with respect to the field of interest representation. These organisations have repeatedly expressed concerns about being subject to the Act without providing exceptions or exemptions (Box 1.13). Several charities have also expressed concern that their status may be challenged if they become subject to the Act. However, the study conducted by the Quebec Commissioner of Lobbying in 2016 had determined that coverage did not pose a problem of consistency with the community action policy or the special status of charities.

Box 1.13. Arguments raised by community organisations against being subject to the Act

Identity and DNA of community organisations

- Non-profit organisations derive their legitimacy from their democratic and political mission and their roots in the community.
- Lobbyists are paid specialists within companies or commercial firms who aim to influence public decision-makers, whereas community organisations are vehicles for social transformation.
- Community organisations do not have pecuniary or corporate objectives; they defend the common good and the general interest.
- The status of lobbyist would not give associations more credibility but would, on the contrary, tarnish their reputation because of the pejorative connotation of the word and the context of the adoption of the law, which was adopted in response to a scandal involving for-profit interests.

Administrative burden and citizen participation

- Registration would be too administratively burdensome and would require additional resources.
- Registration would place registration obligations on volunteers, which would discourage and demobilise volunteers, and threaten the sustainability of these organisations.

Transparency

- Transparency is central to the governance of NPOs (via activity reports, financial statements).
- All the positions and representation activities of community organisations are already made public, often accompanied by a press release.
- A subjugation would lead to an avalanche of registrations in the Lobbyists Registry, the relevance of which is not obvious.

> - The registry would be duplicative, as groups of organisations make the same types of representations as their member organisations, and would contain an overabundance of information.
> - The Act was designed for the private sector in response to a lack of transparency in that sector. There is no real need or risk in making NPOs subject to it.
>
> **Illegitimate government control**
>
> - Being covered by the Act would be an obstacle to the right of association.
> - The desire to force the registration in a public registry of all individuals who engage in political representation activities, without remuneration as lobbyists, is a systematic control of activities emanating from the freedom of association of NPOs.
> - The desire to make NPOs subject to the law is the result of pressure from lobbyists who are subject to the law.
>
> **Policy for the recognition of community action**
>
> - The government would fund organisations to make representations to the State, while requiring these same organisations to register these representations on the register.
> - By their very nature, some organisations meet with the authorities on a frequent basis, and influence communications with public office holders are part of their mission and their DNA in order to position themselves in the public arena.
>
> Source: (Lobbyisme Québec, 2016[11]); Institut du Nouveau Monde (2016), Compte-rendu d'une rencontre organisée par l'Institut du Nouveau Monde sur l'assujettissement des OSBL aux règles d'encadrement du lobbyisme, déposé à l'attention de Me François Casgrain, Commissaire au lobbyisme le 1er mars 2016 ; (Lamarche et al., 2017[28]); Elements shared at the OECD consultation workshop with NPOs on 17 February 2022.

In the continuity of these reflections, the Quebec Commissioner of Lobbying proposed in its Statement of Principles to provide for several exclusions so that the Act ensures a space for dialogue with public institutions.

First, the Commissioner proposes to exclude interest representations made without an intermediaryby a community organisation primarily offering support services directly to the public (Principle 7 of the Statement of Principles). This would exclude community organisations working in the areas of health, the fight against poverty, housing, food aid, autonomy and well-being, family, sports, recreation and culture. This solution, already favoured by the Commissioner in 2016, seems reasonable given the objective sought. Such an exclusion could be included in the same spirit as those existing in Germany, Belgium, Ireland, the United Kingdom and the European Union, which concern the activities of trade unions and social partners as participants in social dialogue.

However, registration requirements could cover groupings of organisations, as part of their mission is to carry out representation activities on behalf of their members. The registration of a grouping or coalition would cover for all members of the grouping. In order to reduce the administrative burden, this requirement should go hand in hand with more flexibility in the registration procedures in the Lobbyists Registry. Only one registration in the Lobbyists Registry per organisation should be required, in which only the names of persons who are salaried or who have been designated to participate in the governing bodies (board of directors) would be indicated, and not those of volunteers, even if they have been mandated to carry out interest representation activities on behalf of the organisation. However, the activities of volunteer members should be monitored and disclosed in the register, without the obligation to register and disclose being placed on these volunteers.

Similarly, it could be clarified that advocacy activities carried out for the benefit of a coalition that has only non-profit members are covered by the Act. Provincial legislation in Alberta, British Columbia, Manitoba, Nova Scotia, Ontario, and Newfoundland and Labrador includes coalitions in the definition of an organisation.

Second, the Quebec Commissioner of Lobbying proposes to define a clear space for dialogue when it is the citizen himself, without an intermediary, who addresses public institutions and when he/she finds himself/herself in a process that already provides for intervention mechanisms or that requires his/her intervention with institutions (for example, to exercise a right or to challenge an obligation imposed by legislation). This would exclude:

- Activities carried out by an entity, in its role as citizen or taxpayer of the State, to promote its own rights or interests if its intervention is specifically provided for or required by law and carried out in accordance with specific processes;
- Activities carried out by an individual or group of individuals to promote their own rights or interests as citizens or taxpayers of the State.

With such an exclusion, communications made by individuals, companies or organisations in order to obtain funding, a permit or an authorisation in a normative context would thus be excluded, since the law or regulation requires the organisation to obtain this permit or authorisation from the State or public institutions.

However, it is necessary to clarify this recommendation to ensure that the registration of these types of organisations in all other cases is not disproportionate to the objective pursued. Indeed, several NPOs reiterated during consultations with the OECD their concerns about the administrative burden of registering as lobbyists in particular cases involving, for example, a single interest representation activity conducted by neighbourhood associations with no employees. For such cases, it seems necessary to consider exemptions in order to preserve the objective of disclosing relevant of information and to avoid imposing a registration obligation on small citizen structures that carry out very little lobbying activity within the meaning of the Act. Certain thresholds could be introduced, and assessed at the level of the entity carrying out activities, such as the time spent preparing, organising, carrying out and following up a lobbying activity. This criterion could be assessed over a period of six months or one year. In British Columbia, for example, thresholds have been introduced where one or more individuals in an organisation, alone or collectively, have spent at least 50 hours lobbying or preparing to lobby in the previous 12 months. A similar mechanism could be envisaged for interest representation activities carried out by an individual, or a group of individuals, where the nature of such representation falls within the scope of the Act. This would both avoid diluting relevance - where such representations are one-off or *ad hoc* - and not totally exclude such activities, which, in the view of several stakeholders interviewed by the OECD, can have considerable influence on certain decisions, particularly at the municipal level.

Finally, interest representation activities carried out by an individual on his or her own behalf and in a non-professional capacity should not be considered lobbying. For example, an individual who writes to a Member of Parliament to request the amendment of a law would not be a lobbyist in the meaning of the Act. This type of exclusion is, inter alia, provided for in Austria ("activities of a person with which he pursues his own non-business interests"), Germany ("activities of natural persons who formulate exclusively personal interests with their submission"), Lithuania ("opinion expressed by a natural person with regard to legislation") and France ("activities of natural persons who carry out interest representation activities for themselves in a non-professional capacity").

The criterion of initiative for lobbying activity is not very relevant and could be removed

In Quebec, section 2 of the Act specifies that a lobbying activity includes any oral or written communication. The arranging by a lobbyist of a meeting between with a public office holder and any other person is considered to be a lobbying activity.

The OECD Recommendation states in Principle 4 that definitions should clearly specify the types of communications that are not considered to be lobbying activities, such as communications that have already been made public, including formal presentations to parliamentary committees, public hearings and established consultation mechanisms.

In addition to the exclusions already specified in Section 1, the Act does not apply to the following activities:

- Representations made in or prior to judicial or adjudicative proceedings ;
- Representations made to a parliamentary committee of the National Assembly or at a public meeting of a municipal council or municipal body ;
- Representations made in public proceedings, or in proceedings that are a matter of public record, to any person or body having jurisdiction or powers conferred by an Act, an order in council or a ministerial order ;
- Any submission the disclosure of which could reasonably be expected to threaten the safety of a lobbyist or a lobbyist's client, a public office holder or any other person.
- Any submission made in response to a written request from a public office holder, including any submission made in response to a call for public tenders issued under the public office holder's authority.

This last exception may make it difficult, in the event of a potential infringement, to trace who initiated a communication, especially when the relationship between a parliamentarian and an interest representative is regular and well established. This also creates inequalities between interest representatives: those who have built up close and regular relationships with decision-makers are more easily identified by public officials and are more often approached; as a result, they may be subject to lesser disclosure obligations than interest groups with limited contacts who almost always initiate these exchanges.

The law could thus specify that the reporting obligation applies when the disclosure is initiated by the public official and does not concern purely factual information. The exception could only concern communications made in response to a request from a public official concerning factual information, as is the case in twelve OECD jurisdictions (Australia, Austria, Belgium, Canada, Chile, France, Germany, Ireland, Peru, the United Kingdom, the United States and the European Union). The Quebec Commissioner of Lobbying had already suggested a similar exception in 2017, recommending that representations made for the sole purpose of answering technical questions from a public office holder be excluded from the application of the Act, provided that the response does not otherwise seek to influence such a decision or cannot be considered as seeking to influence such a decision. In the United Kingdom, a communication from a Minister or Permanent Secretary does not need to be registered. However, if a minister or permanent secretary initiates a communication with an organisation and, as a result of the exchange, the criteria for lobbying are met, the organisation is required to register and record its activity.

Similarly, all representations concerning the execution, interpretation or application of a law or regulation with regard to an organisation could also be excluded. Such a provision exists for example in France (Box 1.14).

> **Box 1.14. Exclusion of communications limited to factual exchanges in France**
>
> In France, not all communications that are limited to factual exchanges are covered by the framework. These are situations where the communication is limited to one of the following purposes:
>
> - Where an organisation requests factual information, accessible to any person, from a public official.
> - When an organisation asks a public official for an interpretation of any existing public decision.
> - When an organisation provides a public official with information about its operations or activities, without a direct link to a public decision, for example in the context of sending an annual activity report or a factory visit.
>
> Source: (HATVP, 2018[29]).

Finally, it seems necessary to maintain the other exceptions provided for, in particular influence communications where all elements of the consultative process are already made public (e.g. hearings in parliamentary committees).

The law should cover grassroots lobbying

Lobbying is itself a constantly evolving concept and the advent of social media has further increased its complexity. Lobbying laws and regulations therefore frame an environment that is bound to change. Increasingly, interest groups are using traditional and social media to shape policy debates, shape public perceptions and those of public officials, or to persuade civil society to put pressure on decision-makers and indirectly influence the public decision-making process. In particular, companies are increasingly using these type of activities to address civil society because of increased expectations of their social and environmental responsibility.

The inclusion of such indirect lobbying activities has become unavoidable. It is also seen by some stakeholders, such as institutional investors, as relevant information that should be disclosed. Indeed, the last decade has seen the emergence in Quebec, as in all OECD jurisdictions, of a new shareholder activism that assesses the contribution of companies to certain societal issues. This "shareholder activism" is also manifested by the demand for greater transparency on companies' political activities (Tchotourian, 2019[30]). Investors and major asset managers increasingly view the lack of transparency on corporate lobbying and political engagement, and its inconsistencies with companies' positioning on environmental and societal issues, as an investment and environmental, social and governance (ESG) performance risk (Principles for Responsible Investment, 2018[31]). The number of shareholder proposals concerning the disclosure of corporate political involvement has increased dramatically over the past decade, becoming one of the most popular types of shareholder resolutions put to the vote, particularly in the area of climate change lobbying (Box 1.15). These proposals systematically include appeals to the general public and indirect lobbying.

> **Box 1.15. The appeal to the general public is seen as relevant information by a growing number of institutional investors and asset managers**
>
> In 2020, BNP Paribas Asset Management submitted proposals in three companies (Chevron, Delta Airlines and United Airlines) requiring them to disclose more information on how their lobbying activities align with the goals of the Paris Agreement. The resolution targeting Chevron received majority shareholder support (54%), while the two other resolutions at Delta and United received 46% and 32% respectively.
>
> In 2021, BNP Paribas Asset Management targeted two companies (Delta Airlines and Exxon Mobil) with a request for more information on how their "lobbying activities (direct and through trade associations) align with the [...] Paris Climate Agreement". The proposal won a majority of votes in both companies (63.8% of votes in Exxon Mobil; Delta has not reported the percentage). In the US, over the course of the 2021 proxy season, three other similar climate-lobbying proposals garnered a majority vote with support levels ranging from 76.4% (Norfolk Southern Corporation) to 62.5% (Phillips66). One proposal, submitted to Sempra Energy, received 38%.
>
> These lobbying proposals required that companies disclose some of the following information on an annual or semi-annual basis:
>
> - Policies and procedures governing direct and indirect lobbying as well as grassroots communications.
> - Expenses made for the purpose of lobbying activities, and the recipients of such payments.
> - Memberships in and payments to any tax-exempt organisation that drafts and endorses legislation.
> - A description of the board and management oversight of lobbying expenditures.
>
> Source: (OECD/PRI, 2022[32]).

Currently, lobbying disclosures in Quebec for registered lobbyists must indicate the types of communication that the lobbyist intends to use or has used. The registry therefore makes it possible to know whether communications will be made through written or oral communications, through physical meetings or telephone calls.

At the international level, the Canadian Lobbyists Registry and the EU Transparency Registry require lobbyists to disclose information on the use of social networks as a lobbying tool. At the federal level, lobbyists are required to disclose any communication techniques used, including grassroots communications. Similarly, the EU transparency register covers activities aimed at "indirectly influencing" the EU institutions, including through organising communication campaigns, platforms, networks and grassroots initiatives. At the sub-national level, most Canadian and US jurisdictions that regulate influence communications consider appeals to the general public as a means of communication to influence public office holders.

As is the case at the federal level and in other Canadian provinces that regulate lobbying activities, the Quebec legislation should also require lobbyists to declare whether they intend to use "grassroots lobbying" as a means of communication. These types of appeals, made directly by a lobbyist to the public or through a widely circulated media, are intended to convince the public, members of an organisation or another group of people with similar interests to communicate directly with a public office holder in order to pressure him or her to support a certain position. Quebec could for example align its Act with the federal requirements (Box 1.16). The Act could also state that signing and requesting signatures on petitions is not covered by this type of communication.

> **Box 1.16. Office of the Commissioner of Lobbying of Canada Interpretation Bulletin on the application of the Lobbying Act to calls to the general public**
>
> In Canada, the Lobbying Act defines "grassroots lobbying" as "any appeals to members of the public through the mass media or by direct communication that seek to persuade those members of the public to communicate directly with a public office holder in an attempt to place pressure on the public office holder to endorse a particular opinion".
>
> In its August 2017 Interpretation Bulletin, the Office of Commissioner of Lobbying of Canada clarified the means used for the purpose of appealing to the general public, which may include letter and electronic messaging campaigns, advertisements, websites, social media posts and platforms such as Facebook, Twitter, LinkedIn, Snapchat, YouTube, etc.
>
> The Commissioner also indicated that participation in the strategic and operational activities of an appeal to the general public (approving items, providing advice, conducting research and analysis, writing messages, preparing content, disseminating content, interacting with members of the public) also requires registration.
>
> Source: (Office of the Commissioner of Lobbying of Canada, 2017[33]).

The Act could require the disclosure of the sources of funding for research, think tanks and organisations

One way in which vested interests influence government policy is by funding third-party organisations, such as think tanks, research institutions or associations. The aim is to present expert opinion, evidence and data and to mobilise the public around the public policy process. However, as with any other form of lobbying, there is a risk of subjective influence, hence the importance of ensuring transparency around these practices to allow for public scrutiny (Benamouzig and Cortinas, 2019[34]; Bruckner, n.d.[35]).

Greater transparency on the funding of these organisations in particular would help to distinguish between genuine advocacy networks and the practice of 'astroturfing'. Astroturfing is the practice of creating or funding citizens' associations or organisations in order to create or reinforce an impression of widespread popular support for a public action or programme, in order to indirectly influence decision making. The messages conveyed give the appearance of a spontaneous and disinterested consumer or citizen movement, but in reality conceal positions aligned with those advocated by an industry, lobby group or other interest group. To date, the EU Transparency Register is the only transparency regime that requires think tanks, research centres and academic institutions to declare the source of their funding: any organisation must indicate its sources of funding in the register, either by providing a link to a web page containing the relevant information or by requiring disclosure of this information to the register if the information is not already publicly available.

The Quebec Act could therefore also cover these indirect lobbying practices, by placing the disclosure obligation on the entities that finance these types of organisations, or by requiring the organisations themselves to disclose their source of funding, as is required at the European level.

The minimum threshold of lobbying activities is a source of confusion and could be removed or assessed at the entity level

As at the federal level, the definition of an enterprise lobbyist and an organisation lobbyist subject to the Act includes the notion of "significant part of duties", indicating the threshold from which influence communications must be disclosed. The Quebec Commissioner of Lobbying has produced several interpretation notices to help lobbyists determine whether they are carrying on activities "for a significant part of duties", but these notices have been challenged in the past before the courts (Cour d'appel du Québec, 2017[36]). The Commissioner is of the opinion that this notion is confusing for both lobbyists and public officials because of its subjective dimension. This aspect of the Act could also allow some lobbyists to circumvent the Act and use this provision as a defence in the event that they are under investigation for not registering their activities.

The Commissioner of Lobbying recommends that "no minimum threshold of activity is required, nor do interest representatives need to be remunerated for the Act to apply" (Principle 5 of the Statement of Principles). Difficulties with the concept of "significant part of duties" have also been noted by other international jurisdictions, such as France and Canada, as well as in other Canadian jurisdictions. Recommendations to remove the substantial part of duties provisions have been made by the Commissioner of Lobbying at the federal level (Office of the Commissioner of Lobbying of Canada, 2020[37]) and in other Canadian jurisdictions.

The recommendation seems consistent with the objective of the Act to make transparent all communications aimed at influencing decisions made by public institutions, and not only those that are carried out for a significant part of duties. However, removing the notion completely could result in a large number of small businesses or organisations having to register for anecdotal or *ad hoc* activities. As discussed above, it seems necessary to provide for more precise thresholds for these particular cases. At a minimum, the Quebec legislator could also consider providing that the status of lobbyist is assessed by considering all of the activities of the legal person concerned, and not those of the natural persons that make up the legal person, in order to determine more relevant thresholds triggering an obligation to register. Such provisions apply, for example, in British Columbia (Box 1.17).

Box 1.17. The notion of threshold in British Columbia

In British Columbia, new provisions that came into force in 2020 require all organisations (including corporations) employing in-house lobbyists to register in the Lobbyists Registry. The only exception to this rule is for organisations with fewer than six employees that lobby on a limited basis.

However, the law provides that an individual is not an in-house lobbyist if he or she meets a threefold in-house criterion, including the threshold concept applied at the entity level:

1. The individual is an employee, director or officer of an organization that has fewer than six employees.

   AND

2. The individual's lobbying - alone or with other individuals in the organisation - on behalf of the organisation or an affiliate of the organisation, totals less than 50 hours in the preceding 12-month period.

   EXCEPT IF

3. The main purpose of the organisation is to represent the interests of its members, or to promote or oppose any issue, and the lobbying carried out by the individual is for that purpose.

For example, if an organisation has fewer than six employees, but one or more individuals, alone or collectively, have spent 50 hours lobbying or preparing to lobby in the previous 12 months, the organisation's lobbying activities must be registered.

Source: Office of the Registrar of Lobbyists of British Columbia, Guidance for organizations, https://www.lobbyistsregistrar.bc.ca/handlers/DocumentHandler.ashx?DocumentID=343

The Act could include provisions on the participation of lobbyists in certain advisory groups

An advisory or expert group refers to any committee, council, commission, congress, panel, working group, similar group or sub-group belonging to it, providing advice, expertise and recommendations to governments. Such groups are composed of members of the public and private sectors as well as representatives of civil society, and may be established by the executive, legislative or judicial branches of government. Individual OECD governments rely heavily on such groups to design and implement public policy. In the context of the COVID-19 crisis, many governments established specially tailored institutional arrangements to provide scientific advice and technical expertise to guide their emergency response and relief plans.

Advisory groups have the potential to strengthen evidence-based decision-making. However, without sufficient transparency and safeguards against conflicts of interest, these bodies face concerns that can undermine the legitimacy of their advice. Indeed, private sector representatives participating in these groups have direct access to policy-making processes without being considered as external lobbyists and may (unconsciously or not) favour the interests of their company/industry, thus contributing to the amplification of conflicts of interest.

In Quebec, consultation with persons having expertise in a particular field is often sought through advisory committees that may be composed of both public office holders and persons representing, among others, businesses, associations or other non-profit groups. In a 2009 opinion, the Quebec Commissioner of Lobbying considered that the exception in section 5 of the Act, which provides that the Act does not apply to representations made in response to a written request from a public office holder, also applies to communications made in the context of the work of an advisory committee established by a public authority, even if the purpose of these communications is to influence the decision-making of the institution in question (Lobbyisme Québec, 2009[38]).

However, in view of the risks, the Act could include a separate exception for advisory functions performed by certain lobbyists to government, specifying certain conditions for the application of this exception. In Ireland, for example, working groups involving members of the private sector must comply with a Transparency Code in order to be exempt from the requirement to register for lobbying (Box 1.18).

> **Box 1.18. Transparency Code for working groups in Ireland**
>
> In Ireland, a working group set up by a Minister or public service body, which consists of at least one designated public official (DPO) and at least one person from outside the public service, and which reviews, assesses or analyses any issue of public policy with a view to reporting to the Minister of the Government or the public service body on it, must comply with a Transparency Code.
>
> The following information must be published on the public body's website upon its establishment:
>
> - Names of Chairperson and Members, together with details of their employing organisation (if they are representing a group of stakeholders, this should be stated).
> - Whether any non-public servant members were previously designated public officials.
> - Terms of reference of the group.
> - Expected timeframe for the group to conclude its work.
> - Reporting arrangements.
>
> In addition, the agenda and minutes of each meeting must be published and updated at least every four months.
>
> The Chairperson must include with the final or annual report of the Group a statement confirming its compliance with the Transparency Code.
>
> If the requirements of the Code are not adhered to, interactions within the group are considered as a lobbying activity under the Regulation of Lobbying Act 2015.
>
> Source: (OECD, 2021[1]).

The Act could also include additional provisions on other communications made by a person who participates in the work of an advisory committee, to the extent that they qualify as lobbying activities within the meaning of the Act. In 2017, the Quebec Commissioner of Lobbying proposed that such communications remain subject to its application:

- If they are made outside the framework of the committee's work.
- If they concern a subject that is outside the committee's mandate or the agenda of a meeting.
- If they are intended to influence the object or scope of the committee's mandate or the content of an agenda and no formal and explicit request to that effect has been made by a public office holder.

In addition, and although not directly related to transparency issues, a balanced representation of interests (if applicable) between private sector and public service representatives and the collection of expertise from different sectors would help to ensure equity and diversity in the advisory group. For example, Norway's Ministry of Local Government and Modernisation has published guidelines on the use of independent advisory groups, which states that the composition of such groups should reflect different interests, experiences and views (Ministère de l'administration locale et de la modernisation de la Norvège, 2019[39]). There is also a need to adopt rules of procedure for such groups, including conditions for appointment, standards of conduct and, in particular, procedures for preventing and managing conflicts of interest. These measures would provide reasonable protection against interest groups undertaking to extract or provide biased advice to government.

Proposals for action

In order to adapt the legislative and regulatory framework to the socio-political and administrative context of Quebec, and to be as consistent as possible with international best practices, the OECD recommends that Quebec considers the following proposals.

Modernising the legal framework in its objectives and terminology

- Section 1 of the Act could include a principle of equitable access to public decision-makers.
- The Quebec legislator could reflect on the terminology used to qualify lobbying activities.

Adapting the scope of the Act

- The scope of public decisions covered could include all stages of the legislative, regulatory, strategic or administrative policy development cycle.
- The Act could allow for greater adaptation of the disclosure requirements for lobbying activities for certain public decisions without a general scope and according to the institutional levels concerned.
- The Act could take into account the advances in transparency and integrity allowed by the Act respecting contracting by public bodies.
- To strengthen the coherence of the scope of application, the Act could also cover the education network.
- The Act could cover all lobbying activities that are carried out with any elected official, officer or staff member of the public institutions covered by the scope.

Provide a robust definition of the terms "lobbying" and "lobbyist

- The Act could make transparent the activities of all interest groups that engage in lobbying activities without providing for exceptions depending on the nature of the organisations.
- The Act could, however, provide for some specific exemptions that take into account the diversity of non-profit organisations, their capacities and resources.
- The criterion of initiative for a lobbying activity is not very relevant and could be removed.
- The Act should cover grassroots lobbying.
- The Act could require the disclosure of the sources of funding for research, think tanks and organisations.
- The minimum threshold of lobbying activities is confusing and could be removed or assessed at the entity level.
- The Act could include provisions on the participation of lobbyists in certain advisory group work.

References

Bégin, L., P. Brodeur and P. Lalonde (2016), "Rapport du Comité public de suivi des recommandations de la Commission Charbonneau", *Éthique et scandales publics*, Vol. 18/2, https://doi.org/10.4000/ethiquepublique.2789. [4]

Benamouzig, D. and J. Cortinas (2019), "Les stratégies politiques des entreprises en santé publique : le cas de l'agroalimentaire en France", *Revue française des affaires sociales*, Vol. 1/3, p. 189, https://doi.org/10.3917/rfas.193.0189. [34]

Bruckner, D. (n.d.), *Fake News: Distortion of Democracy by Opaque, Deceptive and Fake 'Think Tanks'*, Transparify, https://commons.lib.jmu.edu/cgi/viewcontent.cgi?article=1502&context=honors201019. [35]

Colli, F. and J. Adriaensen (2018), "Lobbying the state or the market? A framework to study civil society organizations' strategic behavior", *Regulation & Governance*, https://doi.org/10.1111/rego.12227. [24]

Commission d'enquête sur l'octroi et la gestion des contrats publics dans l'industrie de la construction (2015), *Rapport final de la Commission d'enquête sur l'octroi et la gestion des contrats publics dans l'industrie de la construction*, http://www.bibliotheque.assnat.qc.ca/guides/fr/les-commissions-d-enquete-au-quebec-depuis-1867/7732-commission-charbonneau-2015. [3]

Communication & Institutions (2020), *"Sourcing" des amendements: où en est-on? L'exemple de la loi économie circulaire*, https://www.cominst.com/fr/actualites-ci-lobbying/le-sourcing-des-amendements-dans-la-loi-economie-circulaire-en-un-coup-doeil/. [25]

Cour d'appel du Québec (2017), *Décision Cliche*, http://t.soquij.ca/Ms82A. [36]

Darut, A. and M. Germond (2021), *Lobbying & plaidoyer environnementaux: les juemeaux vénitiens?*, https://www.plaidoyer-lobbying.fr/etude-au-format-pdf/. [15]

Department of Public Expenditure and Reform (2020), *Second Statutory Review of the Regulation of Lobbying Act 2015.*, https://www.gov.ie/en/publication/7ef279-second-statutory-review-of-the-regulation-of-lobbying-act-2015/. [26]

Edelman (2021), *2021 Edelman Trust Barometer: Canada*, https://www.edelman.ca/trust-barometer/edelman-trust-barometer-2021. [5]

Gouvernement du Québec (2001), *L'action communautaire : une contribution essentielle à l'exercice de la citoyenneté et au développement social du Québec*, https://www.mtess.gouv.qc.ca/sacais/action-communautaire/politique-reconnaissance-soutien.asp#:~:text=Politique%20gouvernementale%20sur%20l'action%20communautaire,-L'%C3%A9laboration%20de&text=Par%20cette%20politique%2C%20le%20gouvernement,et%20leur%20pou. [18]

HATVP (2021), *L'encadrement de la représentation d'intérêts. Bilan, enjeux de l'extension du répertoire à l'échelon local et propositions*, https://www.hatvp.fr/wordpress/wp-content/uploads/2021/11/HATVP_Rapport_lobbying_web_2021-VF.pdf. [19]

HATVP (2018), *Répertoire des représentants d'intérêts: Lignes directrices*, https://www.hatvp.fr/wordpress/wp-content/uploads/2018/10/Lignes-directrices-octobre-2018.pdf. [29]

Hepburn, E. (2017), *The Scottish Lobbying Register: Engaging with Stakeholders. A Report by Eve Hepburn prepared for the Scottish Lobbying Register Working Group of the Scottish Parliament*, https://archive2021.parliament.scot/LobbyingRegister/Hepburn_Lobbying_Register_Report_2017_Nov2017.pdf. [27]

Lamarche, L. et al. (2017), *La surveillance et le contrôle technocratique des organismes sans but lucratif (OSBL) : un enjeu de droits collectifs*, https://liguedesdroits.ca/wp-content/fichiers/rapport_droit_association.pdf. [28]

Légis Québec (2002), *Lobbying Transparency and Ethics Act*, https://www.legisquebec.gouv.qc.ca/en/document/cs/T-11.011. [7]

Lobbyisme Québec (2019), *Simplicité, Clarté, Pertinence, Efficacité. Réforme de l'encadrement du lobbyisme*, https://www.commissairelobby.qc.ca/fileadmin/Centre_de_documentation/Documentation_institutionnelle/2019-06-13_Enonce-principes-CLQ.pdf. [8]

Lobbyisme Québec (2017), *La révision de la loi sur la transparence et l'éthique en matière de lobbyisme. Le temps est à l'action. Amendements proposés au projet de loi no 56*, https://www.commissairelobby.qc.ca/fileadmin/user_upload/128_presentation_des_amendements_au_projet_de_loi_no_56.pdf. [12]

Lobbyisme Québec (2016), *Étude sur l'assujettissement de tous les organismes à but non lucratif aux règles d'encadrement du lobbyisme, tel que prévu au projet de loi n°56, Loi sur la transparence en matière de lobbyisme*, https://www.commissairelobby.qc.ca/fileadmin/user_upload/243_etude_obnl_web.pdf. [11]

Lobbyisme Québec (2012), *Proposition de modifications à la Loi sur la transparence et l'éthique en matière de lobbyisme du Commissaire au Lobbyisme du Québec*, https://www.commissairelobby.qc.ca/fileadmin/user_upload/rapport_propositions_modifications_loi_2012.pdf. [10]

Lobbyisme Québec (2009), *Avis no 2009-01, Les activités de lobbyisme faites dans le cadre de travaux d'un comité consultatif institué par une autorité publique et l'application du paragraphe 10o de l'article 5 de la Loi sur la transparence et l'éthique en matière de lobbyisme*. [38]

Lobbyisme Québec (2008), *Bâtir la Confiance. Rapport du Commissaire au Lobbyisme du Québec concernant la révision quinquennale de la Loi sur la transparence et l'éthique en matière de lobbyisme*, https://lobbyisme.quebec/fileadmin/user_upload/277_batir_confiance_rapport_commissaire_lobbyisme_quebec.pdf. [9]

Ministère de l'administration locale et de la modernisation de la Norvège (2019), *Le travail des comités dans l'État. Un guide pour les dirigeants, les membres et les secrétaires des commissions d'études gouvernementales.*, https://www.regjeringen.no/contentassets/793636d2e55a4236b82e632897f96d50/utvalgsarbeid-i-staten_veileder.pdf. [39]

National Conference of State Legislatures (2021), *How States define Lobbying and Lobbyist*, https://www.ncsl.org/research/ethics/50-state-chart-lobby-definitions.aspx#:~:text=States%20generally%20define%20lobbying%20as,either%20written%20or%20oral%20communication.&text=The%20definition%20of%20a%20lobbyist,behalf%20of%20another%20for%20compensati. [17]

OECD (2021), *Lobbying in the 21st Century: Transparency, Integrity and Access*, OECD Publishing, Paris, https://doi.org/10.1787/c6d8eff8-en. [1]

OECD (2020), *Integrity Review of Public Procurement in Quebec, Canada: A Strategic Approach to Corruption Risks*, OECD Publishing, Paris, https://doi.org/10.1787/g2g95000-en. [22]

OECD (2017), *Integrity Framework for Public Investment*, OECD Public Governance Reviews, OECD Publishing, Paris, https://doi.org/10.1787/9789264251762-en. [23]

OECD (2017), *OECD Recommendation of the Council on Public Integrity*, http://www.oecd.org/gov/ethics/OECD-Recommendation-Public-Integrity.pdf. [21]

OECD (2017), *Preventing Policy Capture: Integrity in Public Decision Making*, OECD Public Governance Reviews, Éditions OCDE, Paris, https://doi.org/10.1787/9789264065239-en. [2]

OECD (2017), *Recommendation of the Council on Open Government*, https://legalinstruments.oecd.org/en/instruments/OECD-LEGAL-0438. [13]

OECD (2015), *Recommendation of the Council on Public Procurement*, https://legalinstruments.oecd.org/en/instruments/OECD-LEGAL-0411. [20]

OECD (2010), *OECD Recommendation on Principles for Transparency and Integrity in Lobbying*, https://www.oecd.org/corruption/ethics/Lobbying-Brochure.pdf. [6]

OECD/PRI (2022), *Regulating corporate political engagement: trends, challenges and the role for investors*, OECD Publishing, Paris, https://www.oecd.org/governance/ethics/regulating-corporate-political-engagement.htm. [32]

Office of the Commissioner of Lobbying of Canada (2020), *Annual report 2019-20*, https://lobbycanada.gc.ca/en/reports-and-publications/annual-report-2019-20/. [37]

Office of the Commissioner of Lobbying of Canada (2017), *Applicability of the Lobbying Act to Grass-roots Communications*, https://lobbycanada.gc.ca/en/rules/the-lobbying-act/advice-and-interpretation-lobbying-act/applicability-of-the-lobbying-act-to-grass-roots-communications/. [33]

Ouimet, M., É. Montigny and S. Jacob (2019), "Les pratiques d'encadrement du lobbyisme : Revue systématique de la portée et étude Delphi", *Département de science politique, Université Laval. Cahier de Recherche Électorale et Parlementaire*, Vol. Numéro 18, http://www.cms.fss.ulaval.ca/recherche/upload/chaire_democratie/fichiers/120017_cahier_de_recherche_chaire_democratie_no182.pdf. [14]

Principles for Responsible Investment (2018), *Converging on Climate Lobbying. Aligning Corporate Practice Within Investor Expectations*, https://www.unpri.org/Uploads/g/v/q/PRI_Converging_on_climate_lobbying.pdf. [31]

Sunlight Foundation (2013), *The Landscape of Municipal Lobbying Data*, https://sunlightfoundation.com/2013/04/04/the-landscape-of-municipal-lobbying-data/. [16]

Tchotourian, I. (2019), "Entreprises à mission sociétale : regard de juristes sur une institutionnalisation de la RSE", *Vie & sciences de l'entreprise*, Vol. 2/208, pp. pp. . 72-93, https://www.cairn.info/revue-vie-et-sciences-de-l-entreprise-2019-2-page-72.htm. [30]

Notes

[1] In line with the OECD Recommendation on Principles for Transparency and Integrity in Lobbying, the report uses the term "lobbying". "Lobbying" and the French term "lobbyisme", more commonly used in Quebec, are considered by the OECD to be equivalent.

[2] Since February 17, 2022, "Lobbyisme Québec" designates in French the organisation placed under the authority of the Commissioner of Lobbying, a person designated by the National Assembly, whose appointment must be approved by two-thirds of the members of the National Assembly. The organisation was previously known in French as "Commissaire au Lobbyisme du Québec". In English, "Commissioner of Lobbying" is used to designate both the organisation and the designated person.

2 An approach to transparency of lobbying activities based on the relevance of the information declared

This chapter highlights the challenges that Quebec must meet in order to improve the transparency of the information disclosed in the Lobbyists Registry and to allow for public scrutiny over the policy development process. First, the chapter analyses the registration process and suggests ways to improve the content and granularity of the information declared by lobbyists in the registry. The chapter also discusses how to maximise the technological environment of the Lobbyists Registry as a vehicle for transparency and compliance. Second, the sharing of responsibilities for transparency between lobbyists and public officials is also discussed. Lastly, the chapter provides recommendations for the effective implementation of disclosure requirements and regular review of their application, in order to best meet stakeholder expectations and developments in lobbying.

Introduction

Transparency is the disclosure and subsequent accessibility of relevant public data and information (OECD, 2017[1]). It is a tool for public scrutiny of the policy-making process. The *OECD Recommendation on Principles for Transparency and Integrity in Lobbying* (hereafter "the Recommendation") therefore encourages countries and jurisdictions to provide an adequate degree of transparency to ensure that public officials, citizens and businesses can obtain sufficient information on lobbying activities (Principle 5), while taking into account the administrative burden of compliance, so that this does not become an impediment to fair and equitable access to government. (Principle 2). In particular, jurisdictions are encouraged to facilitate the monitoring of lobbying activities by stakeholders, including civil society organisations, businesses, the media and the general public (Principle 6) (OECD, 2010[2]).

In Quebec, transparency of lobbying activities is provided through the registration of persons making influence communications in the Lobbyists Registry. In order to fully achieve the objective of transparency of influence communications set out in section 1 of the Act, The Quebec Commissioner of Lobbying considers that the relevance of the information declared in the Lobbyists Registry must be a pillar of any future reform of the Act, while preserving a balance between transparency requirements and the reality of lobbying activities.

Furthermore, transparency objectives cannot be achieved if disclosure requirements are not respected by the actors concerned and properly implemented by the supervisory bodies. The OECD Recommendation therefore calls on countries to implement a coherent spectrum of strategies and practices to achieve compliance with transparency measures (Principle 9). The Recommendation also calls on countries to periodically review the application of their lobbying rules and guidelines and make necessary adjustments in light of experience (Principle 10).

This chapter analyses the transparency of information on lobbying in Quebec. Specifically, it examines the procedures for registering in the Lobbyists Registry, the relevance of the information declared, the technological environment as a vehicle for transparency and accountability, and the strategies implemented to ensure compliance with the transparency rules. The chapter also discusses mechanisms for raising awareness of the expected rules and standards, as well as the periodic review of the transparency framework to allow for adjustments in light of experience.

Clarify registration and disclosure procedures for all actors involved

The OECD Recommendation states that the public has a right to know how public institutions and public officials made their decisions, including, where appropriate, who lobbied on relevant issues (Principle 6 of the Recommendation). It also states that information on lobbying activities and lobbyists should be stored in a publicly available register (Principle 5 of the Recommendation). In order to achieve this objective, it is important to clarify the registration and disclosure requirements for actors subject to transparency obligations, including:

- Registration as a prerequisite for the exercise of any lobbying activity.
- Registration deadlines.
- The persons or entities responsible for registration.
- Possible adjustments to take account of the scale and nature of the lobbying sector.

The Act could specify that timely registration should be a prerequisite for any lobbying activity

Currently, any lobbyist covered by the Lobbying Transparency and Ethics Act must register in the Lobbyists Registry. This provision allows the Québec regime to be in line with international best practices. Indeed, voluntary registries or initiatives by lobbyists' associations remain limited in their impact (OECD, 2021[3]; OECD, 2014[4]). In most OECD countries that have established a transparency register, the registration of lobbyists is mandatory to conduct lobbying activities. Where registration is voluntary, such as in the Netherlands or the European Union, registration is required for access to certain public officials or public buildings, such as parliament. Similarly, in all US and Canadian jurisdictions that have instituted a transparency register, registration is also mandatory.

Currently, section 25 of the Act states that no person may lobby a public office holder without being registered in the registry of lobbyists in respect of such lobbying activities. Returns to the registry are made based on the duration of lobbying activities, corresponding to a period covered by the lobbying activities, which must include the name of any parliamentary, government or municipal institution in which any public office holder is employed or serves with whom the lobbyist has communicated or expects to communicate, as well as the ministerial, deputy-ministerial, managerial, professional or other nature of the functions of the public office holder;

In its Statement of Principles, the Quebec Commissioner of Lobbying considers that all individuals and entities must be required to register in the disclosure system established by the Act if they wish to carry out lobbying activities with or without an intermediary (Principle 8 of the Statement of Principles). This implies that entities and individuals wishing to engage in lobbying activities must register at the stage of intending to engage in such activities, and not after they have done so or within a limited time frame.

To pursue this objective, section 25 of the Act could be clarified to provide that a lobbyist may only engage in these activities if he or she is registered in the registry in respect of these activities within the time and in the manner prescribed by the Act or by regulation. These clarifications are essential in order to clarify the role of public office holders, particularly with respect to the verification that the lobbyist who lobbies the office holder complies with his or her obligation to disclose the activities in the Lobbyists Registry. Section 25 could also specify that a lobbying activity may only be carried out if the name of the public institution for which the public office holder with whom the lobbyist intends to communicate or has communicated is registered by the lobbyist within the prescribed time. This proposal, already considered by the Quebec Commissioner of Lobbying in its previous recommendations, would not only ensure timely access to such information, but also provide public officials with clear guidance on the interactions they are allowed to have with lobbyists. This aspect will be covered in Chapter 3.

The Act could reduce and harmonise registration deadlines for all lobbyists

Currently, the Quebec Lobbyists Registry is based on the principle of disclosure of the intent to conduct lobbying activities. Section 14 of the Act specifies different registration deadlines for consultant lobbyists and organisation lobbyists. In the case of a consultant lobbyist, registration must be made no later than the thirtieth day after the day on which the lobbyist begins to lobby on behalf of a client. In the case of an enterprise lobbyist or an organisation lobbyist, the deadline is 60 days.

These registration deadlines could be an obstacle to the objective of transparency and timely access to registration information, and could also be confusing for some public office holders who may wish to verify a lobbyist's registration before entering into communication with him or her (this issue will be addressed in Chapter 3). Several elected officials and leaders of public institutions interviewed by the Quebec Commissioner of Lobbying in 2018 raised the need to shorten the registration period, so that the lobbyist's registration can be verified before a meeting or within a few days of the interaction.

The Act could impose a shorter registration period, and apply the same period to all lobbyists, which could be derived from good practices in other Canadian jurisdictions, such as British Columbia's Lobbying Act, Newfoundland and Labrador's Act, and Toronto's and Ottawa's municipal systems (Table 2.1). This harmonisation of registration deadlines is also recommended by the Office of the Commissioner of Lobbying of Canada to improve transparency, ensure that all registrations are made in a timely manner and increase fairness between different categories of lobbyists (Office of the Commissioner of Lobbying of Canada, 2021[5]).

Table 2.1. Registration deadlines in Canadian provinces and some municipalities

Jurisdiction	Registration deadlines for consultant lobbyists	Registration deadlines for in-house lobbyists
Canada (federal law)	10 days	2 months
British Columbia	10 days	10 days
Alberta	10 days	2 months
Saskatchewan	10 days	60 days
Manitoba	10 days	2 months
Ontario	10 days	2 months
Quebec	30 days	60 days
New-Brunswick	15 days	2 months
Prince Edward Island	10 days	2 months
New England	10 days	2 months
Newfoundland and Labrador	10 days	10 days
Yukon	15 days	60 days
City of Ottawa	15 working days	15 working days
City of Toronto	3 working days	3 working days

Source: (Office of the Commissioner of Lobbying of Canada, 2021[5]).

The registry should place the obligation to register on entities, not individuals, while including the identity of each lobbyist

In Quebec, registration is made, in the case of a consultant lobbyist, by the lobbyist himself and, in the case of an enterprise lobbyist or an organisation lobbyist, by the senior officer of the enterprise or group on whose behalf a lobbyist is acting. However, the registration of more than one enterprise lobbyist or organisation lobbyist may be done by filing a single return containing the information pertaining to each of these lobbyists. The current Act therefore places all the obligations related to the transparency of their activities on individuals, without recognizing that these activities are carried out for the benefit of an enterprise, an organisation or another individual. Furthermore, the records filed in the registry by consultant lobbyists are filed in the name of the lobbyist and not in the name of the corporation that was mandated to carry out the lobbying activities.

In its Statement of principles, the Quebec Commissioner of Lobbying proposes to assign the represented entities the responsibility of authorising any interest representative to carry out lobbying activities on its behalf and of ensuring the disclosure, truthfulness, reliability and follow-up of lobbying activities performed by their in-house interest representatives (Principle 9 of the Statement of Principles), and to assign external interest representatives the responsibility of ensuring the disclosure, truthfulness, reliability and follow-up of lobbying activities made on behalf of their clients (Principle 10 of the Statement of Principles). This proposal would, on the one hand, make external interest representatives - as legal persons, except in the case of an individual acting as an independent lobbyist - responsible for disclosing all activities carried out on behalf of their clients, which is already provided for in the law, and on the other hand, place the responsibility for registration, disclosure and monitoring of all lobbying activities on legal persons.

This proposal would ensure better access to the information contained in the register. To this end, entities can be designated by a unique identifier or reference number. Such a unique reference is also foreseen in the new registration platform being developed by the Quebec Commissioner of Lobbying, which was inspired by the approach adopted in France (Box 2.1). According to the draft terms and conditions of the Lobbyists Registry, any enterprise or organisation will have to have a "collective space" when an enterprise or organisation lobbyist engages in lobbying activities on its behalf; similarly, any consultant lobbyist's enterprise will have to have its collective space. To create this collective space, the Quebec enterprise number assigned by the *Enterprise Register of Quebec* must be used (Lobbyisme Québec, 2019[6]).

Box 2.1. Registration of interest representatives in France

In France, interest representatives must communicate their identity to the High Authority for Transparency in Public Life by entering their SIREN number (national company identifier) or their identification number in the national register of associations (RNA) in the teleservice provided for registration. If they do not have either of these two numbers, they can contact the High Authority's services via the teleservice to communicate their identity and be given an identification number to register.

Next, the names of the legal representatives who have the necessary prerogatives to act on behalf of the organisation and represent it in relation to third parties, whether or not they carry out interest representation activities, must be communicated to the High Authority. The identity of persons considered to be "in charge of interest representation activities" within a legal person is also recorded.

Finally, for interest representatives who carry out activities wholly or partly on behalf of third parties, the clients for whom interest representation activities are carried out must be disclosed.

Source: HATVP, https://www.hatvp.fr/espacedeclarant/representant-dinterets/ressources/#post_4620.

These new arrangements for registering entities in the registry should make it easier to find accurate information about entities in the registry, whether the activities are registered by an in-house lobbyist or by an external lobbyist, and to avoid duplication.

In keeping with these developments, it will be important that any future review of the Act be able to shift the registration requirement from individuals to entities. This will further reduce the administrative burden of registration by allowing all entities employing enterprise, organisation or consultant lobbyists to designate a registrar to consolidate, harmonise and report on the activities of the entity. The Act could also maintain the obligation to disclose in the registry the names of all individuals who have engaged in lobbying activities. Such a disclosure regime would also allow an entity to be held accountable for potential breaches of the Act. This aspect is discussed later in the chapter.

The Act could give entities the option of assuming responsibility for reporting lobbying activities carried out by their member entities

Under the current Act, when an organisation adopts strategic orientations that are then the subject of lobbying activities with public institutions by the member entities of that organisation, each member entity must register those activities in the registry, which can create numerous duplications in the registry. In its discussions with several organisations subject to the Act, the Quebec Commissioner of Lobbying has noted the difficulties encountered by groups of organisations and the need to simplify disclosure requirements. In its Statement of Principles, the Commissioner recommends the implementation of an "umbrella disclosure", allowing an entity to disclose, for a specific mandate, the entirety of the lobbying activities undertaken by the individuals or entities that are its members, by assuming, on their behalf, the responsibility for and conformity of the lobbying activities (Principle 20 of the Statement of Principles). For example, an entity could report all activities of its subsidiaries or related entities. In the case of NPOs, federations, trade union organisations and groupings of organisations, whose primary mandate is to represent their members, could also report lobbying activities for their members.

However, this measure must be clarified to avoid any risk of regulatory loopholes. First, the Act should clarify that this umbrella disclosure should only apply to interest representation that is coordinated and/or determined at the level of the entity that brings together member entities. All other lobbying activities that are coordinated by a particular member on its own behalf should be subject to disclosure by that specific entity, not by the entity of which it is a member.

Secondly, the Act could require the umbrella entity to disclose on behalf of which specific interests or members the lobbying activities are being carried out. Indeed, it is generally accepted that organisations such as federations or business associations lobby on behalf of all their members. However, in practice, there may be an unwritten rule among members that allows some companies to lobby for their positions when key regulatory issues in their sector are discussed, and this often results in the most active and vocal members' views being adopted, even if they are sometimes in the minority. Therefore, it seems essential to strengthen the disclosure rules of umbrella organisations so that the specific beneficiaries of an advocated position that may represent minority interests within such an entity are disclosed, so that minority interests are not misrepresented as those of the general membership.

Thirdly, the Act could require that umbrella entities must contain the names of the organisations that form the entity; member entities, when registering, should also indicate in the register the organisations of which they are members, which could facilitate cross-checking information in the register. Such a provision exists for example in France, which requires all interest representatives to disclose "the professional or trade union organisations or associations related to the interests represented" to which they belong.

Lastly, the Act should clarify that the obligation to register umbrella entities applies regardless of the number or status of the employees of that entity. Currently, the Act covers coalitions and groupings to the extent that they are organisations formed for employer, trade union or professional purposes or if their members are predominantly for-profit companies. As specified in Chapter 1, all coalitions should be required to register when they engage in lobbying activities. The Act could clarify that this principle applies even to coalitions that do not have full-time employees. Similar recommendations have been made in Ireland by the Standards in Public Office Commission, which oversees the Lobbying Act, regarding the registration of coalitions and interest groups representing commercial interests (Box 2.2).

> **Box 2.2. Irish recommendations on communications by unpaid persons who hold office in bodies representing professional and/or business interests**
>
> In Ireland, representative bodies and coalitions representing professional and/or business interests are only covered by the Lobbying Act if they have one or more full-time employees.
>
> However, the Standards in Public Office Commission has noted that there are a number of representative bodies that exist primarily to represent the interests of their members, but do not have full-time employees and are therefore not subject to the Act. This means that some bodies/associations that regularly communicate with public office holders are not covered by the Act, despite the fact that in some cases their members would fall within the scope. Organisations that represent members who are therefore independently within the scope of the law are able to avoid the registration requirement, simply because the representative body has no employees.
>
> The Commission has also noted a number of cases where informal coalitions of business interests have been formed to lobby as a group on an issue of mutual interest to the industry. These informal coalitions usually have a name but in most cases do not have employees. The Commission found examples of such coalitions in the airline sector, software companies and in the entertainment and leisure sector. In such circumstances, where the coalition has no employees, it is not necessary for it to register.
>
> Whether or not these coalitions or informal bodies were formed with the intention of circumventing the provisions of the law, their lobbying activities fall outside the scope of the law and are not made transparent. The Commission has made several recommendations that any business representative body or 'coalition' of business interests, regardless of the number or status of employees, should fall within the scope of the Act, provided that one or more of the members of the body or coalition would fall within the scope if they were acting themselves. The Commission also considers that the members of the body/coalition should be required to be named in the declarations in order to promote greater transparency.
>
> Source: Standards in Public Office Commission, 2019 Legislative Review of the Regulation of Lobbying Act 2015: Submission by the Standards in Public Office Commission, https://www.lobbying.ie/about-us/legislation/2019-legislative-review-of-the-regulation-of-lobbying-act-2015-submission-by-the-standards-in-public-office-commission/.

The registration of non-profit organisations should not include the names of volunteers engaged in lobbying activities

The OECD Recommendation states that basic disclosure requirements should take into account the scale and nature of the lobbying sector, particularly where there is limited supply and demand for professional lobbying, and the administrative burden of compliance, so that this does not become an obstacle to fair access to the administration (Principle 2 of the Recommendation). While non-profit organisations active at federal and provincial level often have departments dedicated to lobbying, communication and public relations activities, this is not necessarily the case for small local organisations.

In order to clarify registration requirements for non-profit organisations, registration could be simplified with regard to the disclosure of the names of individuals engaged in lobbying activities. The registration should only disclose the names of individuals who are employees or who have been appointed to participate in the governing bodies (for example the board of directors), who would be responsible for ensuring the disclosure, veracity, monitoring and centralisation of lobbying activities carried out on behalf of the entity. Lobbying activities carried out by volunteers should be tracked and recorded without the names of the individuals acting as volunteers appearing in the register.

Strengthening the content of information reported to the register

The OECD Recommendation states that disclosure of lobbying activities should provide sufficient, pertinent information on key aspects of lobbying activities to enable public scrutiny. In order to adequately serve the public interest, the Recommendation states that information on lobbying activities and lobbyists should be stored in a publicly available register and regularly updated to provide accurate information for effective analysis by public officials, citizens and businesses (Principle 5 of the Recommendation). To achieve this objective, the Quebec legislator may consider the following key elements

- The expectations of various stakeholders (citizens, public decision-makers, companies, shareholders, journalists, researchers) to better delimit the disclosure regime.
- The basic disclosure requirements enabling public officials, citizens and businesses to obtain sufficient information on lobbying activities.
- Measures to monitor lobbying activities through a system of regular disclosures.

The Quebec legislator could take into account the expectations of various stakeholders in order to define a relevant disclosure regime

The OECD Recommendation provides a set of guidelines for delineating core disclosure obligations as well as supplementary information taking into account legitimate information needs of key players in the public decision-making process (Principle 5 of the Recommendation). From this perspective, the expectations expressed in Quebec and internationally provide guidance on what is in the public interest to make transparent in a disclosure regime.

The OECD's interviews with various stakeholders revealed a consensus on the need to supplement the information currently reported to the registry, particularly on the targets of lobbying and the amounts invested. On the citizen side, interviews and focus groups conducted by the Quebec Commissioner of Lobbying in 2018 to develop the Statement of Principles revealed a growing demand to identify elected officials, managers or staff of public institutions who have been the target of lobbying activities. Some researchers interviewed by the OECD regretted that they could not assess, for example, the number of meetings between representatives of a specific industry and the ministry concerned over a given period of time, by comparing it with the number of meetings obtained by non-profit organisations on the same issues. Similarly, some journalists stressed the relevance of obtaining information on the amount of money invested annually in lobbying, in order to appreciate and compare the size of the lobbying sector in certain industries. Most of the stakeholders interviewed also stressed the need to indicate the specific decisions targeted by lobbying activities, in order to ensure the traceability of the public decision.

It is generally assumed that professional lobbyists oppose the creation of lobbying registers and the public disclosure of their lobbying activities. However, many lobbyists surveyed by the OECD in 2020[3] expressed a willingness to participate in a mandatory lobbyist registry, and many felt that this was necessary to protect the integrity of the profession (OECD, 2014[4]; OECD, 2021[3]). These attitudes reflect a commitment to integrity in public decision-making and the importance of maintaining public trust (Figure 2.1).

Figure 2.1. Best means for regulating lobbying, according to lobbyists

Respondents were asked the following question: "In your opinion, which is the best means for regulating lobbying activities?"

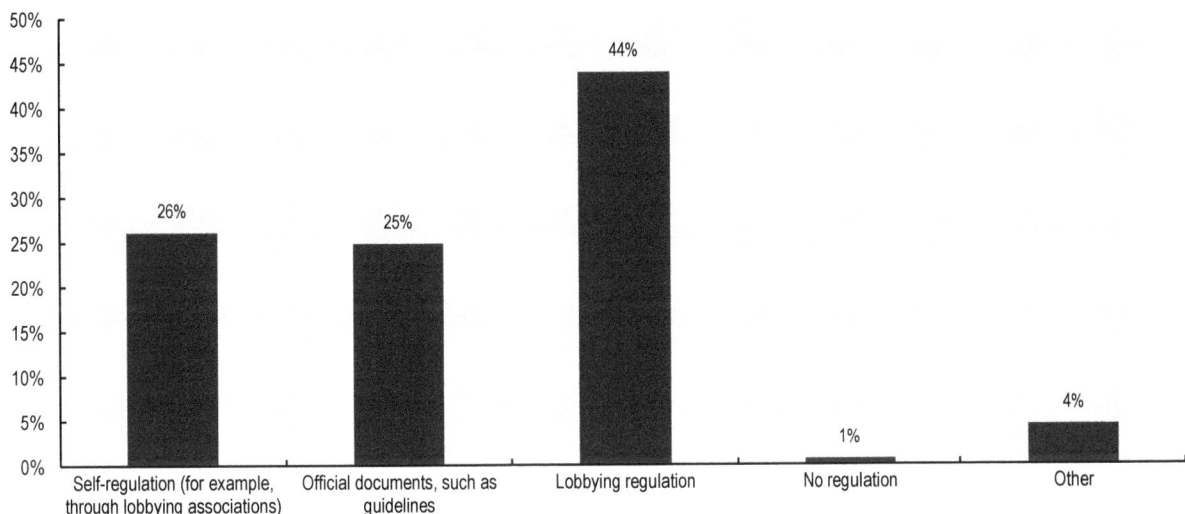

Source: Enquête de l'OCDE sur le lobbying (2020).

The same lobbyists surveyed by the OECD in 2020 were 71% of the opinion that lobbyists' contributions to political party funding should be made transparent (Figure 2.2). However, several Quebec lobbyists stressed in discussions with the OECD the need to strike a balance between making relevant information available to the public and protecting confidential information; legitimate exemptions should be considered to preserve certain information in the public interest or to protect commercially sensitive information if necessary.

Figure 2.2. In OECD countries, lobbyists favour disclosure of political campaigns contributions when registering lobbying activities

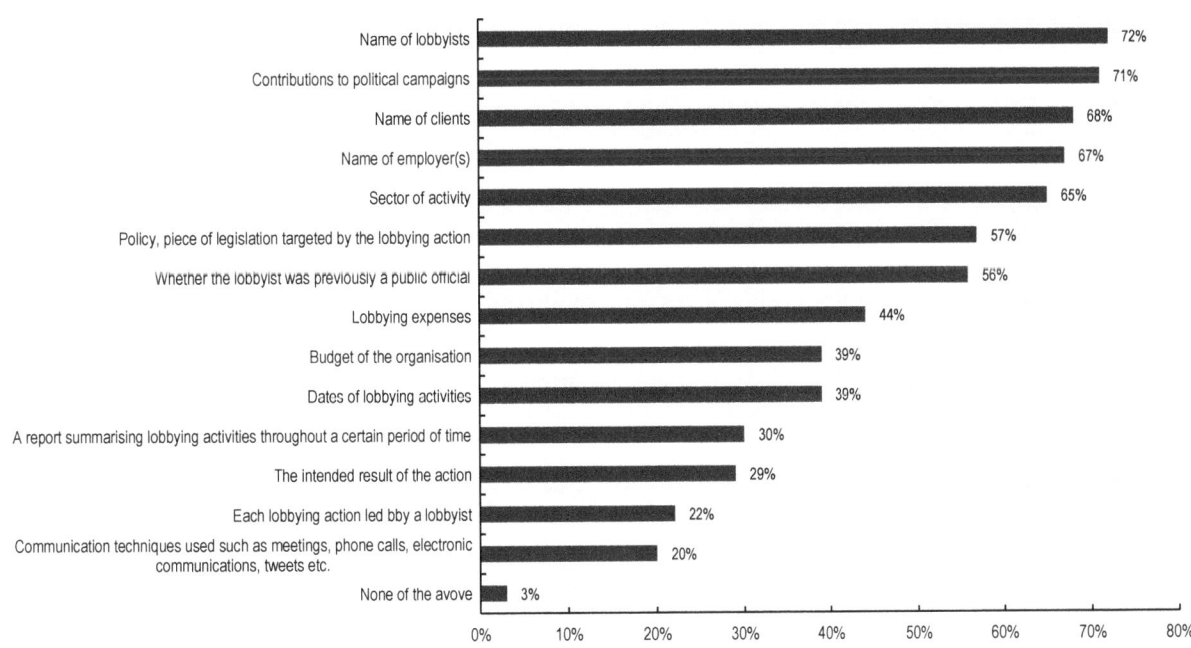

Source: OECD 2020 Survey on Lobbying.

Examining a company's lobbying activities has also become an increasingly common practice by some shareholders or institutional investors, as discussed in Chapter 1. For example, some shareholders of listed companies have become particularly active in recent years in passing resolutions that require increased transparency of lobbying activities. The content of these resolutions gives an indication of what is not always required in transparency registers but is considered relevant by these actors. In most cases, shareholders request disclosure of lobbying activities carried out, including any indirect lobbying or grassroots communications, as well as the amounts allocated to these activities (Ceres, 2021[7]; Principles for Responsible Investment, 2018[8]; Glass Lewis, 2021[9]).

Finally, interviews conducted by the Quebec Commissioner of Lobbying with parliamentary and municipal elected officials in 2018 showed that while they adhere to the principle of transparency of lobbying activities, some municipal elected officials stressed that transparency could compromise certain benefits. The OECD's interviews with parliamentarians confirmed these trends. The elected officials interviewed highlighted the undeniable progress made by the Lobbyists Registry, and the majority supported disclosure of the purpose of any lobbying activity, while expressing some reservations about the extent of information that should be declared so as not to increase the administrative burden or lead to an overabundance of information.

The current reporting obligations only imperfectly meet the transparency objectives of the Act and would benefit from being clarified to include the objective pursued and the public decision targeted

The OECD Recommendation states that core disclosure requirements should elicit information on in-house and consultant lobbyists, capture the objective of lobbying activity, identify its beneficiaries, in particular the ordering party, and point to those public offices that are its targets. Supplementary disclosure requirements might shed light on where lobbying pressures and funding come from (Principle 5 of the Recommendation). In other words, the OECD Recommendation encourages the disclosure of information on who is lobbying, on what and how (Table 2.2).

In his Statement of Principles, the Quebec Commissioner of Lobbying proposes to require all relevant information to be disclosed, including the identity of interest representatives and entities undertaking or benefiting from lobbying activities, public institutions targeted and all information, financial or otherwise, that is deemed relevant for understanding the goals of a lobbying activity and the means used to carry it out (Principle 17 of the Statement of Principles).

Currently, the Lobbying Transparency and Ethics Act already covers some of these elements and is therefore in line with international best practices. Returns in the registry are made in the form of "time periods" covered by lobbying activities. The Act requires the disclosure of the identity of the lobbyist and his or her employer, the subject matter and purpose of the lobbying activities, as well as the public institutions targeted by the lobbying activities and the means of communication that the lobbyists intend to use. The Act also requires disclosure of any person, corporation, subsidiary or association, who, to the knowledge of the lobbyist, controls or directs the activities of the client (in the case of a consultant lobbyist) and/or the employer (in the case of a consultant lobbyist and an organisation or enterprise lobbyist) and has a direct interest in the outcome of the lobbyist's activities. This provision could be complemented by the disclosure of any affiliation with a coalition or professional association, as well as the name of each member - where the member is a corporation - of such organisations, as they may also benefit from the lobbying activities (this recommendation is elaborated above). Finally, the Act requires the disclosure any financial compensation received by consultant lobbyists, by tranche of amounts paid.

Table 2.2. Who undertakes lobbying activities, on what and how?

Information to shed light on lobbying activities	Lobbying Transparency and Ethics Act
WHO - Information on lobbyists and beneficiaries	
Name of lobbyists	✓
If the lobbyist was previously a public official	✓
Name of lobbyists' employer	✓
Business sector or sector of activities	X
Names of clients, if any	✓
Parent or subsidiary company benefiting from the lobbying activities	✓
Name of any members or affiliation with an association/organisation	X
Public funding received	✓
WHAT - Objectives, decisions and targeted agents	
Targeted legislation, proposals, decisions or regulations	X
Identity of the targeted public institutions	✓
Type of public official targeted (general nature of duties)	✓
Identity of targeted public officials	X
Subject matter of lobbying activities	✓
Objectives and desired outcomes	✓
Objectives and results achieved	X
HOW - Details of communications or meetings with public officials	
Financial information	✓
Communications and lobbying techniques used	✓
Overview of lobbying actions undertaken	✓
Each lobbying action undertaken	X
Specific date and/or location of communications	X
Political contributions	X

Notes : In the case of Quebec, the financial amounts dedicated to lobbying activities are only disclosed in the case of a consultant lobbyist. Lobbyists must select a range in which the amount or value of what has been received or will be received for lobbying activities falls: less than USD 10 000, USD 10 000 to USD 50 000, USD 50 000 to USD 100 000 and USD 100 000 or more.
Source: (Légis Québec, 2002[10]).

Although the Interpretation bulletin 2012-01 of the Commissioner of Lobbying requires lobbyists to provide sufficient details in relation to the time period and public decisions targeted (Lobbyisme Québec, 2012[11]), the Act does not explicitly require the disclosure of certain information that would help identify the specific public decisions being targeted. Nor is it required to specify the number of meetings or the frequency with which communications take place. This is because the Act requires the disclosure of lobbying activities at the stage of intent. Journalists interviewed for this report pointed out that the Lobbyists Registry at the federal level provides more information on the dates and target of lobbying activities, while the Quebec legal framework only requires a window of dates that is often too broad. Similarly, citizens interviewed in 2018 by the Quebec Commissioner of Lobbying pointed out that the disclosure of financial amounts at the stage of the intention of lobbying activities, and not of completed activities, could mislead them into believing that the lobbying activity had been carried out, whereas the amount is only an estimate.

In sum, the initial declaration could be simplified, for example by removing information that is not relevant at the stage of the intention to lobby, such as financial amounts. More precise information, such as the dates of lobbying activities, and the specific public officials and decisions targeted, could be required in regular updates, in order to allow citizens to fully grasp the scope and depth of these activities.

The initial return could also include information that is currently not disclosed but which may give relevant indications on the different means that can be mobilised for lobbying activities. For example, the disclosure of public funding received could be extended to any type of funding received, in order to shed light on the so-called *astroturfing* practices discussed in Chapter 1. Following the same model as the European Union, this disclosure should allow entities to provide either a link to an existing webpage providing information on funding received, or to detail this information in the register if it does not exist in the public domain. A similar recommendation had already been made by the Quebec Commissioner of Lobbying in 2012. The recommendation stated that a lobbyist's return should indicate the name of any person, enterprise or organisation that contributes, financially or otherwise, to a lobbying activity, as entities may have an interest in the lobbying activities of an interest group by contributing financially without having control or direction over the activities of that interest group.

The Act could provide for monitoring of lobbying activities by implementing regular disclosure mechanisms to ensure timely access to information on lobbying

The OECD Recommendation recalls that to adequately serve the public interest, disclosure on lobbying activities and lobbyists should be updated in a timely manner in order to provide accurate information that allows effective analysis by public officials, citizens and businesses. (Principle 5 of the Recommendation). In Quebec, regular disclosures are limited to an update of the information contained in the initial return (Table 2.3).

Table 2.3. Updating and renewal of the information of the initial return in Quebec

	Current deadlines
Registration renewal (consultant lobbyist)	30 days after the anniversary date of the first registration
Registration renewal (enterprise lobbyist or organisation lobbyist)	60 days after the end of the financial year
In the event of a change in the content of a lobbyist's declaration (e.g. termination of his or her engagement, taking up new activities)	30 days (notice of change)

Source: (Légis Québec, 2002[10]).

This lack of monitoring can be particularly problematic as disclosures are made at the stage of intent. It may hamper the possibility of public scrutiny, as the information disclosed does not allow stakeholders to monitor lobbying activities or to obtain precise indications of the activities that were effectively carried out, which are the only ones that have an impact on the public decision targeted. The declaration of intent in the initial declaration should therefore be followed up more closely, to validate whether the activity has taken place, been postponed or simply not followed up. In its Statement of Principles, the Quebec Commissioner of Lobbying recommends requiring the disclosure of any intention to undertake lobbying activities and the follow-up of any activity undertaken, especially if an elected official or an officer designated by a public institution is being lobbied (Principle 19 of the Statement of Principles).

In order to simplify the registry and reduce the administrative burden on the one hand, while improving the granularity of information on the other, Quebec could consider providing for a simplified initial registration, complemented by a requirement to publish regular activity reports on all lobbying activities conducted with an elected official or designated officer of a public institution. In Canada, for example, the requirement for lobbyists to publish monthly communications reports has resulted in the prompt publication of information on lobbying activities related to COVID-19 and the identification of the objectives of the lobbying activities as well as the policies and public officials targeted (Box 2.3).

> **Box 2.3. In Canada, the regular publication of communication reports has allowed for the timely disclosure of information**
>
> Recognising that "Canadians have a right to know who has communicated with the country's decision-makers during this unprecedented period" of COVID-19, the Office of the Commissioner of Lobbying of Canada has not granted any extensions and has issued regular reminders, including through social networks. In May 2020, the Office of the Commissioner of Lobbying of Canada also added a new feature to the Online Registry of Lobbyists, allowing users to view lobbying registrations related to COVID-19. The tool searches for the criteria "COVID-19", "COVID", "coronavirus" and "pandemic" in the subject line details of all lobbying registrations. Users can then filter the information by type of activity, topic and public institution targeted, and access the associated monthly communications reports. The Office has also issued guidelines on COVID-19 registration and emergency funding requirements to advise lobbyists whether an application for a federal funding program related to COVID-19 should be published, as well as the periods for updating the information.
>
> Source: (Office of the Commissioner of Lobbying of Canada, 2020[12]).

The Quebec Commissioner of Lobbying recognised, however, that this type of requirement adds a considerable administrative burden to interest representatives and would be difficult to apply in Quebec, where the Act also covers the municipal level, the health and social services network and, potentially, the education network, as well as several non-profit organisations. Regular disclosure could thus be envisaged on a quarterly or semi-annual basis, as is the case in Ireland or the United States, for example (Table 2.4). The Commissioner had previously recommended in 2017 that lobbyists be required to declare, every three months, no later than January 15, April 15, July 15 and October 15, the results of their lobbying activities for the last quarter, in accordance with the procedures determined by the Commissioner. (Lobbyisme Québec, 2017[13]).

Table 2.4. Frequency of disclosure of communications and meetings between lobbyists and public officials in selected countries

	Initial registration	Updating and subsequent recording of information on lobbying activities
Canada	Lobbyists' registration is **mandatory** to conduct lobbying activities: • Consultant lobbyists must register within 10 days of entering an agreement to lobby. • In-house lobbyists must register when they meet a threshold ("significant part of duties") and have 60 days to register.	Information must be updated **every six months**. If a communication has been made with a "designated public office holder", a "**Monthly return**" must be filed, including: 1. The **name of the designated public office holder** who was the object of the communication 2. The **date** of the communication. 3. **Subject-matter** of the communication. When lobbying activities are carried out on behalf of a new client, the client's identity must be registered within one month. Lobbyists must file "annual activity reports", submitted within three months of the end of the lobbyist's financial year.
France	Lobbyists' registration is **mandatory** to conduct lobbying activities. Registration must be done within two months of the start of lobbying activities.	Lobbyists must file "**annual activity reports**", submitted within three months of the end of the lobbyist's financial year. The report contains the following information: 1. Types of **public decisions** targeted by lobbying activities. 2. **Type of lobbying activities undertaken**. 3. **Issues** covered by these activities, identified by their purpose and area of intervention. 4. **Categories of public officials** the lobbyist has communicated with.

	Initial registration	Updating and subsequent recording of information on lobbying activities
Ireland	Lobbyists' registration is **mandatory** to conduct lobbying activities. Lobbyists can register after commencing lobbying, provided that they register and submit a return of lobbying activity within 21 days of the end of the first "relevant period" in which they begin lobbying (The relevant period is the four months ending on the last day of April, August and December each year).	5. The identity of **third parties**. 6. The amount of **expenditure** related to lobbying activities in the past year, identified by thresholds. The 'returns' of lobbying activities are made at the end of each 'relevant period', **every four months**. They are published as soon as they are submitted and contain the following elements: 1. Information relating to the **client** (name, address, main activities, contact details, registration number). 2. The **designated public officials** to whom the communications concerned were made and the body by which they are employed. 3. The **relevant matter** of those communications and the results they were intended to secure. 4. The **type and extent** of the lobbying activities, including any "**grassroots communications**", where an organisation instructs its members or supporters to contact DPOs on a particular matter. 5. The **name** of the individual who had primary responsibility for carrying on the lobbying activities. 6. The name of each person who is or has been a designated public official employed by, or providing services to, the registered person and who was engaged in carrying on lobbying activities.
United States	Lobbyists' registration is **mandatory** to conduct lobbying activities. Registration is required within 45 days: (i) of the date lobbyist is employed or retained to make a lobbying contact on behalf of a client; (ii) of the date an in-house lobbyist makes a second lobbying contact.	Lobbyists must file **quarterly reports** on lobbying activities and semi-annual reports on political contributions. Quarterly reports on lobbying activities (LD-2), include: 1. Specific issues on which the lobbyist(s) engaged in lobbying activities. 2. Houses of Congress and specific Federal Agencies contacted. 3. Disclosing the lobbyists who had any activity in the general issue area.

Source: Recherches complémentaires par le Secrétariat de l'OCDE.

The content of regular disclosures could include the specific decision being targeted, the names of certain public officials designated as "designated officials" who have been the subject of an influence communication, as well as financial information on the resources allocated to lobbying activities. This type of identification of designated officials is already present in several Canadian jurisdictions, including at the federal level (Table 2.5).

Table 2.5. Monitoring of representations made to elected or designated officials in Canadian jurisdictions with lobbying legislations in place

Interest representatives must state whether they have made, or plan to make, representations to…

	Member of Parliament	Minister	Staff member of a public institution
Canada (Federal level)	○	●	●
Alberta	●	●	●
British Columbia	●	●	●
Prince Edward Island	●	○	●
New Brunswick	●	○	●
New England	●	○	●
Ontario	●	●	●
Saskatchewan	●	●	●
Newfoundland and Labrador[1]	●	○	●
Yukon[2]	●	●	●
Manitoba	○	○	○
Quebec	○	○	○

	Member of Parliament	Minister	Staff member of a public institution
● Yes	9	6	10
○ No	3	6	2

1. In addition to members of the City Council of the City of St. John's.
2. In addition to deputy heads as defined in the Public Service Act.
Source: (Lobbyisme Québec, 2019[14]).

In most of these jurisdictions, there is a clear delineation of which public office holders are subject to these additional disclosure obligations, based on the nature of their duties or the degree of decision-making power they have. Canada is an example: if contact has taken place with a "designated public office holder", the interaction must be recorded in the Lobbyists Registry on a monthly basis, in a detailed "Monthly Communication Report", and include the names of the individuals contacted, the location of the meeting and the topics discussed during the exchange. The Quebec legislator could reflect on the categories of public office holders who could be concerned by additional disclosure obligations. In any case, it is recommended that the list of "designated public officials" be precisely delimited, publicly accessible and kept up to date. In Ireland, for example, each public body is required to publish and maintain a list of designated public officers under the Lobbying Act 2015; the Standards in Public Office Commission also publishes a list of public bodies with designated public officers on the lobbying website (Box 2.4). The Quebec Commissioner of Lobbying has already taken steps in this direction, as the new platform includes a list of specific functions adapted according to the level of government (parliamentary, governmental, organisations, municipal).

> **Box 2.4. Obligation to publish a list of designated public officials in Ireland**
>
> In Ireland, Section 6(4) of the Lobbying Act 2015 requires each public body to publish a list showing the name, rank and brief details of the role and responsibilities of each 'designated public official' of the body. This list must be kept up to date. The purpose of the list is twofold:
>
> - To enable members of the public to identify individuals who are designated public officials; and
> - To serve as a resource for lobbyists filing a return with the registry who may need to find contact information for a designated official.
>
> The list of designated public officials should be prominently displayed and easily found on the home page of each organisation's website. This page should also contain a link to the lobbying register http://www.lobbying.ie.
>
> Source: Standards in Public Office Commission, Requirements for public bodies, https://www.lobbying.ie/help-resources/information-for-public-bodies/requirements-for-public-bodies/.

In order to promote compliance and registration, the Quebec Commissioner of Lobbying could propose guidelines for lobbyists to monitor their lobbying activities. Such guidelines, in the form of monitoring guidance, exist for example in British Columbia and France (Box 2.5).

> **Box 2.5. "How to trace your lobbying activities" tool developed by the HATVP in France**
>
> Pursuant to Article 3 of Decree No. 2017-867 of 9 May 2017 on the digital directory of interest representatives, the latter are required to send the High Authority for Transparency in Public Life details of the activities carried out over the year within three months of the close of their accounting period. This annual declaration takes the form of a consolidated report by subject and declared in the form of returns on the disclosure platform.
>
> **Designate a "referent" responsible for consolidating, harmonising and declaring the activity returns in the teleservice**
>
> Designating a "referent" person, such as the organisation's operational contact, has several advantages: (i) the consolidation of representation actions is centralised and facilitated; (ii) the title of the objects is harmonised and therefore more coherent and intelligible; (iii) as the referent is previously trained on the directory, this avoids confusion and misinterpretation of the scope of application of the system; (iv) the online declaration is carried out by a single person; (v) internally, the organisation's employees have a clearly identified contact person for these issues.
>
> **Identify all persons likely to be qualified as "persons responsible for interest representation activities"**
>
> - Identify *a priori* the persons likely to fall within the scope, on the basis of job titles and the tasks generally carried out.
> - Ask all identified persons to trace their communications with public officials.
> - After a period of six and then twelve months, analyse whether the required threshold has been reached;
> - Register the persons identified in the register and disclose their activities.
>
> **Implement an internal reporting tool**
>
> This tool must allow for the consolidation of all the information that should be included in the annual declaration of activities, in particular:
>
> | | |
> |---|---|
> | Date | Indicate the date or period in which the advocacy action was carried out |
> | Action carried out by | Indicate the name of the person in charge of interest representation activities who initiated the action |
> | Objet | Indicate the objective of the interest representation action, preferably by indicating the title of the public decision concerned and using a verb (e.g. "PACTE law: increase the tax on ...") |
> | Area(s) of intervention | Choose one or more areas of intervention from the 117 proposals (several choices possible, up to a maximum of 5 choices) |
> | Name of the public official(s) requested | Indicate the name of the public official(s) requested |
> | Category of public official(s) requested | Choose the type of public official(s) you want from the list (several choices possible) |
> | Category of public official(s) requested: Member of the Government or ministerial cabinet". | If you have selected "A member of the Government or Cabinet", choose the relevant ministry from the list |
> | Category of public official(s) applied for: Head of independent administrative authority or independent administrative authority | If you have selected "A head of an independent administrative authority or an independent administrative authority (director or secretary general, or their deputy, or member of the college or of a sanctions committee)", choose the authority concerned from the list |
> | Type of interest representation actions | Choose the type of interest representation action carried out from the list (several choices possible) |
> | Time spent | Indicate the time spent in increments of 0.25 of a day worked; 0.5 corresponding to a half day and 1 corresponding to a full day |

Costs incurred	Indiquez tous les coûts liés au travail de représentation (commande d'une étude, invitation à déjeuner, etc.).
Annexes	Attach all necessary supporting documents: cross-reference to diary, working documents, email, expense report, etc.
Observations	Comments (optional)

Source: HATVP, https://www.hatvp.fr/wordpress/wp-content/uploads/2018/09/fiche-pratique-reporting-sept-2018-vf.pdf ; https://www.hatvp.fr/wordpress/wp-content/uploads/2018/09/fiche-pratique-objet-sept-18.pdf.

Lastly, the disclosure of financial information remains a marginal practice in Canada, and Quebec is the only province to require such disclosure with respect to compensation received by consultant lobbyists. However, disclosure of such information remains relevant. In the United States, the amounts spent on lobbying activities are systematically disclosed. In France and in the European transparency register, expenses are also disclosed in categories. In these jurisdictions, the disclosure of such information makes it possible to better measure the size of a certain lobbying sector and to identify imbalances in the forces of influence. The Quebec legislator could therefore consider maintaining this obligation, while extending it to in-house lobbyists of corporations and organisations, as well as to contingent fees, and requiring it only at the stage where the lobbying activities have actually taken place.

The vast majority of American jurisdictions also require the disclosure of any political contribution, financial or otherwise, to political parties or candidates. However, the Quebec Commissioner of Lobbying considers this obligation disproportionate and not a meaningful indicator in the Quebec context, as the legal framework in Quebec imposes a maximum donation of CAD 100 for each elector. As for the disclosure of lobbyists' political activities, the Charbonneau Commission had proposed to "protect the financing of political parties from influence in order to draw a line between legitimate influence relationships in a democratic society and others". The Commission recommended, among other recommendations, that the Election Act specify that volunteer work must at all times be done personally, voluntarily and without consideration and require political entities to disclose in their annual financial report and in their return of election expenses the names of persons who have done volunteer work in the field of expertise for which they are usually remunerated, in order to prevent bogus volunteerism compensated by businesses. Similarly, the Commission recommended combating the use of nominees in political financing, which has allowed some companies to finance provincial and municipal political parties by asking their employees and relatives to make personal contributions that are reimbursed by the company, by requiring the identification of the political contributor's employer in the political parties' returns.

While these measures relate more specifically to electoral laws, political activities of companies or organisations (assimilated to third party interventions) can be considered as lobbying activities, and it may be relevant to include certain information in the register in order to provide clarification on where lobbying pressures and funding come from (Principle 5 of the OECD Recommendation). In addition, the interviews conducted by the OECD confirmed that the intervention of third parties, for example NPOs whose financing is not known, during the pre-election period, could constitute a significant risk. In this perspective, regular disclosures could be requested for political activities outside the election period for companies and organisations that lobby, which are not regulated in Quebec (Box 2.6).

> **Box 2.6. Regulation of partisan interventions by third parties in Quebec**
>
> Within the meaning of the electoral laws, it is prohibited for third-party groups, including any organisation acting neither on behalf of a political party nor on behalf of a candidate (businesses, NPOs, legal persons or partnerships, associations, unions, organisations or groups of persons) to make partisan interventions during an election period. An intervention is considered partisan if it offers visibility to a party or a candidate, for example by promoting or opposing the election of a candidate, and if it generates costs, for example the printing of documents, such as posters or pamphlets, as well as the creation of a website or the purchase of advertisements on social media.
>
> These rules apply in provincial elections, in municipal elections in municipalities with a population of 5 000 or more, and in school elections. For example:
>
> - An individual **may not print posters** promoting a candidate at his or her own expense in the workplace or in any other public place.
> - A business **may not buy an advertisement** in a newspaper to denounce the position of a party or candidate on an issue.
> - A non-profit **organisation cannot post a PDF brochure** that rates the policies of candidates in its municipality on a scale of 1 to 10.
> - A union **cannot pay for a Facebook ad** that promotes or opposes a party or candidate policy.
> - An association **cannot create a website** to support a candidate or party, as there is a cost to creating and maintaining that website.
>
> As of June 10, 2016, the Chief Electoral Officer has the power to claim from a political entity a contribution or part of a contribution for which he or she has convincing evidence that it was made contrary to election laws, regardless of when the contribution was made. In the interest of public transparency, the election laws further provide that the Chief Electoral Officer shall make public on his website, 30 days after the receipt of the claim for contributions to a political entity, various information related to those contributions as of June 10, 2016. Whether or not the political entity has made the repayment is also indicated.
>
> Source: Élections Québec, Intervenir dans le débat électoral, https://www.electionsquebec.qc.ca/francais/municipal/financement-et-depenses-electorales/intervenir-debat-electoral.php.

In sum, more regular monitoring of lobbying activities could be required, while avoiding too tight timetables, which could increase the administrative burden of registration, as well as too extensive timetables, which could lead to disclosure of lobbying activities after the decisions targeted by the activities have been taken, thus altering the timeliness and relevance of information declared.

Maximising the technological environment of the Lobbyists Registry as a vehicle for transparency and accountability

In order to achieve broad stakeholder support for the Act, a key challenge is to design tools and mechanisms for the collection and management of information on lobbying practices, and to publish them in an open and reusable format allowing users to identify trends in the large volumes of data. To this end, it is important to facilitate the registration as well as the monitoring of lobbying activities by stakeholders, including civil society organisations, companies, the media and the general public.

The OECD Recommendation encourages jurisdictions to enable stakeholders – including civil society organisations, businesses, the media and the general public – to scrutinise lobbying activities, including through the use of information and communication technologies, such as the Internet, to make information accessible to the public in a cost-effective manner (Principle 6 of the Recommendation). The Recommendation also encourages providing lobbyists with convenient electronic registration and report-filing systems, facilitating access to relevant documents and consultations by an automatic alert system (Principle 9 of the Recommendation). In this perspective, it is necessary to:

- Maximise the use of disclosure platforms to make the practical reality of lobbying visible.
- Implement incentives for lobbyists when registering, in order to foster a culture of compliance.
- Provide, depending on the resources available, automatic verification mechanisms to strengthen controls.

The Commissioner of Lobbying could maximise the use of the new platform to make the practical reality of lobbying more visible

In its Statement of Principles, the Quebec Commissioner of Lobbying stresses the need to establish a mandatory, public disclosure system for lobbying activities based on open data and providing free access, at all times, to relevant and verifiable information allowing anyone to be aware of and understand the lobbying activities and respond to them in a timely manner (Principle 16 of the Statement of Principles). To this end, online disclosure platforms should allow information to be properly structured to facilitate the understanding of lobbying activities and its analysis by users.

In June 2019, with the adoption of Bill 6, the Quebec Commissioner of Lobbying was given the responsibility of designing and administering a new, simple and effective platform to replace the current registry. This measure responds to the wishes expressed by the Commissioner, which recommended in its Statement of Principles to confer the responsibility and administration of the disclosure system on the Commissioner of Lobbying (Principle 18 of the Statement of Principles). The administration of the registry was previously entrusted to the Office of the Register of personal and movable real rights, under the Department of Justice, which acted as registrar of lobbyists. Above all, this measure is an important step towards easing the regulatory burdens on entities subject to transparency obligations.

Above all, this measure has enabled the Commissioner to initiate a process of revision of the Lobbyists Registry to improve the registration process and the technological environment. The Commissioner is expected to launch a new platform in 2022 to address, among other issues, the technological shortcomings of the current Lobbyists Registry (Box 2.7).

> **Box 2.7. Overview of improvements to the Quebec Lobbyists Registry planned for spring 2022**
>
> For **citizens** and **registry users**, the new platform will include several new features, including:
>
> - A **clearer presentation of mandates** in the form of detailed records, including the lobbyists who carry them out, the public decision-makers they try to influence during a given period, and any updates made.
> - A **news feed** allowing users to follow new registrations and thus to know about ongoing lobbying activities, including in relation to certain themes.
> - A **better performing search tool** allowing advanced searches according to predefined criteria (e.g. search by public institutions, by sector of activity, by registered entity etc.).
> - A **personalised interface experience** with the possibility to create a user account, allowing to save the results of certain searches, to program preferences and to receive notifications according to the programmed preferences.
> - A **lobbying information area**, including lobbying news, international comparisons, institutional announcements or communications, statistical reports.
>
> For **lobbyists**, the platform aims to make registration easier and more efficient:
>
> - **Lobbying activities over a time period can be registered and amended quickly and without delay by authorised persons**. The Commissioner's checks will be ex-post, to allow timely transparency.
> - **Formatted selection fields** will limit the need to manually enter information, while others will be connected to certain public databases (e.g. the Enterprise Register, Légis Québec, etc.) in order to promote the consistency and validity of the information.
> - Lobbyists will have access to a **Professional Space and a Collective Space**, including reporting assistance processes for drafting, monitoring, updating and managing mandates, and allowing the collective drafting of a return before its publication.
> - From their Professional Space, lobbyists will be able to manage their returns **on a simplified dashboard**, which will display their profile, contact information, notifications, the mandates that concern them and the Collective Spaces to which they are attached.
>
> Source: Commissaire au Lobbyisme du Québec, Registre des lobbyistes : aperçu des améliorations, https://lobbyisme.quebec/registre-des-lobbyistes/apercu-des-ameliorations/; Projet de modalités de tenue du registre des lobbyistes https://lobbyisme.quebec/fileadmin/Centre_de_documentation/Documentation_institutionnelle/projet-modalites-tenue-registre-lobbyistes.pdf

To define the contours of this new platform and meet the expectations of various stakeholders, the Quebec Commissioner of Lobbying conducted a public consultation on the terms and conditions of disclosures to the future lobbying disclosure platform, spread over 45 days from May 11 to June 21, 2021. A total of 15 persons submitted comments or questions, including 4 consultant lobbyists, 3 enterprise lobbyists, 5 organisation lobbyists, 1 citizen and 2 public office holders (Lobbyisme Québec, 2021[15]). The Commissioner also relied on a User Committee to provide advice in the development of the future platform, made up of representatives concerned with the regulation of lobbying in Quebec, including lobbyists, public office holders, journalists and individuals acting as citizens (Lobbyisme Québec, n.d.[16]). These efforts to engage all key players are a noteworthy good practice and contribute to a common understanding of the expected disclosure obligations. They also allow the Commissioner to better understand the factors that influence compliance with registration requirements, and to update enforcement strategies and mechanisms accordingly, which is a key principle of the OECD Recommendation (Principle 10 of the

Recommendation). Most importantly, they help to better address the above-mentioned new expectations of various stakeholders regarding the transparency and integrity of lobbying activities.

Depending on the announced functionalities and when operational, this platform would be one of the best practices in force in OECD countries. The lobbying information zone, similar to the "*Tout savoir sur le lobbying*" ("*Everything you should know about lobbying*") platform currently being implemented in France, will mainly document the practical reality of lobbying. The Commissioner has already implemented efforts in this direction, including:

- The publication, every week, of statistics on the evolution of the number of registered lobbyists, active lobbyists, declarations or opinions, enterprises and organisations with at least one active lobbyist, active clients and active returns.
- The sending of a newsletter every Monday ("Info Registre Hebdo"), allowing users to receive the most recent entries registered in the registry, and to obtain information on lobbying activities conducted with parliamentary, governmental and municipal public institutions.
- The sending of a monthly newsletter on lobbying news ("Lobbyscope").

The new platform will allow the Commissioner to pursue these efforts, for example by publishing dashboards and data visualisation systems to facilitate access and understanding of the large volumes of data collected in the registry. The Commissioner will also be able to use the data in the registry to produce targeted analyses on the practical reality of lobbying. In France, for example, the obligation to declare the objective of lobbying activities makes it possible to trace the influence communications made on a specific bill or decision (Box 2.8).

Box 2.8. Thematic analyses on lobbying published by the High Authority for transparency in public life in France

In 2020, the High Authority for the Transparency of Public Life implemented a new platform on lobbying. This platform contains practical factsheets, answers to frequently asked questions, statistics as well as thematic analyses based on data from the register.

For example, the High Authority has published two reports on declared lobbying activities on specific bills, which shed light on the practical reality of lobbying.

Source: HATVP, https://www.hatvp.fr/lobbying.

The registry could include incentive for lobbyists such as automatic reminders of disclosure obligations

Jurisdictions need to find innovative solutions to simplify registration and disclosure mechanisms and foster a culture of compliance. While the existence of a sanctions regime does act as a deterrent, the OECD Recommendation states that enforcement strategies and mechanisms should provide incentives for lobbyists, including automatic alert systems. Sending automatic reminders to lobbyists and public officials about disclosure obligations can help limit the risk of non-compliance (OECD, 2021[3]) (Box 2.9). A similar system could be implemented in Quebec.

> **Box 2.9. Automatic reminders to raise awareness of disclosure deadlines produce results**
>
> **Australia**
>
> Registered organisations and lobbyists receive reminders about mandatory reporting obligations via biannual emails. Registered lobbyists are reminded that they must advise of any changes to their registration details within 10 business days of the change occurring, and confirm their details within 10 business days of 31 January and 30 June each year.
>
> **France**
>
> Interest representatives receive an email fifteen days before the deadline for submitting annual activity reports.
>
> **Germany**
>
> In the absence of updates for more than a year, interest representatives receive an electronic notification requesting them to update the entry. If the information is not updated it within three weeks, the interest representative' is marked as "not updated".
>
> **Ireland**
>
> Registered lobbyists receive automatic alerts at the end of each of the three relevant periods, as well as deadline reminder emails. Return deadlines are also displayed on the Register of Lobbying's main webpage.
>
> **United States**
>
> The Office of the Clerk of the House of Representatives provides an electronic notification service for all registered lobbyists. The service notifies, by email, of future filing deadlines or relevant information regarding disclosure-filing procedures. Reminders on filing deadlines are also displayed on the Lobbying Disclosure Website of the House of Representatives.
>
> Source: (OECD, 2021[3])

The implementation of automatic verifications by the Lobbyists Commissioner could be useful in promoting public scrutiny

The use of data analysis and artificial intelligence can facilitate the verification and review of data, particularly with regard to the section on the objectives pursued by lobbying activities. In France, in addition to the electronic submission of registrations and activity reports, including features to facilitate disclosure, the High Authority for the Transparency of Public Life has implemented an automatic verification mechanism using an artificial intelligence-based algorithm to detect potential flaws in the validation of annual lobbying activity reports (Box 2.10). Given the similarities between the Quebec and French regimes with respect to the section concerning the objectives pursued by lobbying activities, a similar verification system could be implemented by the Commissioner of Lobbying.

> **Box 2.10. Implementation of an algorithm based on artificial intelligence technology to detect potential deficiencies and improve the quality of annual lobbying activity reports**
>
> In France, registered lobbyists must submit an annual activity report to the High Authority for Transparency in Public Life within three months of the lobbyist's financial year. During the analysis of activity reports for the period 1 July 2017 to 31 December 2017, the High Authority noted the poor quality of some of the activity reports due to a lack of understanding of what was expected to be disclosed. Over half of the 6 000 activity reports analysed did not meet any of the expected criteria. Very often, the section describing the issues covered by lobbying activities – identified by their purpose and area of intervention – was used to report on general events, activities or dates of specific meetings.
>
> In January 2019, the High Authority implemented a series of mechanisms to enhance the quality of information declared in activity reports. In addition to the provision of practical guidance explaining how the section on lobbying activities should be filled in and the display of a pop-up window with two good examples of how this section is supposed to be completed, the High Authority implemented an algorithm based on artificial intelligence technology to detect potential defects upon validation of the activity report, and detect incomplete or misleading declarations.
>
> Source: (OECD, 2021[3])

Sharing responsibility for transparency with public decision-makers

The OECD Recommendation encourages jurisdictions to establish principles, rules and procedures that give public officials clear guidance on the relationships they are permitted to have with lobbyists (Principle 7 of the Recommendation). This is elaborated in more detail in Chapter 3. However, these principles could include a sharing of transparency obligations:

- Through public agendas; or
- Through the implementation of the legislative footprint.

The Quebec legislator could consider setting up open agenda initiatives for certain public officials

As in Quebec, the transparency measures introduced by countries generally assign the burden of disclosure to lobbyists through a lobbying registry. An alternative and potentially complementary approach is to assign this responsibility to public officials targeted by lobbying activities, requiring them to disclose information about their meetings with lobbyists, through a registry (Chile, Peru and Slovenia), open agendas (Spain, the United Kingdom and the European Union) and/or by requiring public officials to inform their superiors of their meetings with lobbyists (Hungary, Latvia and Slovenia).

These 'open agenda' policies can include information about a public official's meetings, such as dates and times, stakeholders met and the purpose of the meeting. In countries that combine lobbying registers with open agendas (e.g. the United Kingdom and Romania), cross-checking the agendas and lobbying information from registers can provide an opportunity to further analyse who has tried to influence public officials and how (Box 2.11). In other countries, agendas are made available on request or in special circumstances. In Norway, the Ombudsman has stated that the right of inspection includes access to ministers' personal diaries (OECD, 2021[3]).

> **Box 2.11. Open agendas initiatives in Spain**
>
> In Spain, since 2012, the agendas of elected members of the Government are published online, on the Government website. The agenda lists daily the visits, interventions or meetings in which members of the Government participate. Each item discloses at least:
>
> - The minister in charge, and other minister(s) assisting.
> - The time of the meeting.
> - The organisation met or visited.
>
> In October 2020, the Boards of both Houses of the Spanish Parliament adopted a Code of Conduct for members of the Congress and the Senate, which requires the publication of the Senators' and Deputies' agendas, including their meetings with interest representatives. An agenda section is available on the webpage dedicated to each deputy.
>
> Source: (OECD, 2021[3])

In Quebec, at the moment, the responsibility for transparency rests solely with lobbyists. Only the agenda of ministers is public and more or less detailed: the information is updated every three months, which does not allow for an adequate and timely level of transparency on the dates of the meetings held. Quebec could therefore consider legal reform to encourage public officials to publish their meetings with interest representatives (somewhat lower down the scale, such as cabinet directors and appointed officials). Since the current Lobbyists register does not indicate with whom the meeting took place within the public entity, or indeed whether it actually took place, this information could be relevant. Following the European model, the publication of these meetings, and not of the entire agenda, could be made mandatory for certain public officials: members of the government, members of cabinets, chairpersons of committees within the National Assembly (OECD, 2021[3]).

Disclosure of the normative footprint could also complement the information contained in the Lobbyists Registry

The OECD Recommendation states that governments should also consider facilitating public scrutiny by indicating who has sought to influence legislative or policy-making processes, for example by disclosing a 'legislative footprint' that indicates the lobbyists consulted in the development of legislative initiatives (Principle 6 of the Recommendation). Indeed, in addition to lobbying registers and public agendas, several countries provide transparency on lobbying activities based on *ex post* disclosure of information on how decisions were made. The information disclosed can be in the form of a table or a document listing the identity of the stakeholders contacted, the public officials involved, the purpose and outcome of their meetings, and an assessment of how the inputs received from external stakeholders was taken into account in the final decision.

In Quebec, the new platform will allow lobbyists to indicate a bill from a list of bills taken directly and in real time from the list produced by the National Assembly. This development is an important step in facilitating the legislative footprint. Going further, the disclosure of the legislative footprint by public authorities can indicate whether the position expressed by lobbyists has been taken into account in decision-making. Poland and Latvia have implemented such requirements (Box 2.12).

> **Box 2.12. *Ex post* disclosures of how decisions were made in Poland and Latvia**
>
> **Publication of a legislative footprint in Poland**
>
> Poland provides transparency on lobbying activities through a Register of entities performing professional lobbying activities, as well as lists of registered persons administered by the chambers of Parliament (the Sejm and the Senate). Managers of public authorities must publish, once a year and by the end of February, information on the actions targeting them by lobbyists.
>
> In addition, the Standing Orders of the Sejm (Article 201c) provides for the publication of proposals, expert opinions and legal opinions submitted by lobbyists to Committees working on a specific bill. The documents are made available on the Information System of the Sejm. The Senate Regulations (Article 63) also specify that the rapporteur of a committee reporting on legislation must inform when activities are performed by professional lobbyists during the course of committee work. They must also present the committee's position vis-à-vis the proposals presented by lobbyists.
>
> **Latvia**
>
> In Latvia, employees covered by transparency requirements shall inform the direct manager or the head of the institution regarding any expected meeting with lobbyists, and disclose the information received from lobbyists, including what interests they represent, what proposals were expressed, and in what way they have been considered.
>
> If the proposal expressed by lobbyists is considered when drafting or making a decision, this shall be indicated in the document related to such decision (e.g., in the summary, statement, cover letter) and, where possible, made publicly available.
>
> Source: Additional research by the OECD Secretariat.

Implementing mechanisms for effective implementation and enforcement of disclosure obligations

Compliance is a particular challenge when countries address emerging concerns such as transparency in lobbying. While setting clear and enforceable rules and guidelines is necessary, this alone is insufficient for success. To ensure compliance, and to deter and detect breaches, the OECD Recommendation encourages countries to design and apply a coherent spectrum of strategies and mechanisms, and to ensure that key stakeholders are involved in their implementation (Principle 9 of the Recommendation). These strategies and practices include:

- The allocation of appropriate resources to monitoring and enforcement activities.
- Clarifying the responsibilities of entities for the application of sanctions.
- The application of visible and proportionate sanctions, including traditional financial or administrative sanctions, such as debarment, and criminal prosecution where appropriate.
- The public disclosure of proven breaches of disclosure obligations.
- Mechanisms to raise awareness of the expected rules and standards, to ensure a better understanding of the application of these rules and standards.

The Quebec legislator should ensure that the Commissioner of Lobbying has sufficient powers to carry its duties

The OECD Recommendation states that countries should develop and implement a coherent set of strategies and mechanisms that include the allocation of appropriate resources to monitoring and control operations. The Quebec Commissioner of Lobbying performs this monitoring and investigation function under the jurisdiction of the National Assembly. The Commissioner, the person responsible for administering the control system, enjoys the status of a designated person of the National Assembly, appointed by a two-thirds vote of its members (section 33 of the Act), which guarantees his/her independence of action and the impartiality of his/her decisions.

In its Statement of Principles, the Commissioner of Lobbying recommends to set out the Commissioner of lobbying's duties in a way that ensures impartiality, independence of action and fairness of decisions, and to set out the establishment by the National Assembly of the Commissioner's powers, the appointment, replacement and remuneration procedure as well as the method of financing and accountability for activities (Principle 22 of the Statement of Principles). The Commissioner also recommends to set out the powers and duties for the Commissioner of lobbying that are adapted to the position and consistent with those of other persons designated by the National Assembly (Principle 23 of the Statement of Principles), for example, the obligation to declare under oath before the President of the National Assembly that he/she will carry out his/her functions honestly, impartially and fairly and that he/she will not reveal, without being duly authorised to do so, the information obtained in the exercise of those functions. These two proposals seem reasonable insofar as they make it possible to precisely define the role of the Commissioner, to strengthen the accountability mechanisms, and to better align its mode of operation with that of the other persons designated by the National Assembly.

With respect to the powers of supervision and control, the Commissioner may, pursuant to section 39 of the Act, on the Commissioner's own initiative or on request, conduct inquiries if the Commissioner believes on reasonable grounds that there has been a breach of any provision of this Act or of the code of conduct. He may specially authorise any person to make such enquiries. The Commissioner may also act or authorise any person to act as an inspector to determine whether the legislative provisions or the provisions of the code of conduct are being complied with. The person acting as an inspector may:

- Enter, at any reasonable time, the establishment of a lobbyist or a public office holder or the establishment where the lobbyist or the public office holder engages in his or her activities or exercises his or her functions ;
- Require the persons present to provide any information concerning the activities engaged in or the functions exercised by the lobbyist or the public office holder, and to produce any book, register, account, record or other related document ; and
- Examine and make copies of documents containing information relating to the activities engaged in or the functions exercised by the lobbyist or the public office holder (Section 41 of the Act).

In discussions with the OECD, the Commissioner of Lobbying's teams indicated that they have sufficient resources to carry out the functions currently assigned to them by the Act. For the 2020-2021 fiscal year, the Commissioner of Lobbying had a budget with a total appropriation of USD 5 920 362 and an expenditure budget of USD 4 154 039. The Commissioner's staff are appointed in accordance with the Public Service Act (Table 2.6).

Table 2.6. Structure and number of employees of the Quebec Commissioner of Lobbying

Direction	Number of employees as of 4 March 2022
Office of the Commissioner	7
Audit and Investigations Directorate	12
Directorate of Institutional Affairs and Communications	13*
Legal Affairs and Customer Service Directorate	12
Total	**44**

*Excluding the Director, who is already accounted for in the Commissioner's Office and has three positions being staffed.
Source: Information provided by Lobbyisme Québec.

The Commissioner further recommends that the Commissioner of lobbying and the persons the Commissioner designates, maintain the powers and protection for commissioners appointed under the Act respecting public inquiry commissions, as well as the powers of inquiry, verification and inspection, and introduces the power to make formal demands to provide information, in addition to the power to publish certain reports and recommendations or penalties when deemed relevant for the purposes of the Act (Principle 24 of the Statement of Principles). Currently, if the person or entity being interviewed refuses to provide certain documents electronically, investigators must travel to the site and consult the documents in question. For this reason, the Commissioner believes that this power, which is found in other Canadian jurisdictions such as Ontario and British Columbia, could improve the efficiency of its investigation processes.

Lastly, the Commissioner has also recommended prescribing the requirements for keeping information on lobbying activities for verification and inquiry purposes. (Principle 13 of the Statement of Principles). The Commissioner takes the example of other pieces of legislation in Quebec, where there is a regulatory power to require the retention of documents that are directly related to the activities concerned, and relies on the Directive respecting the management of procurement contracts, service contracts and construction contracts of public bodies.

It will be up to the Quebec legislator to ensure, in light of the experience accumulated over the past twenty years, that the Quebec Commissioner of Lobbying has sufficient powers of investigation and control to carry out its missions.

The Act could provide for entity-level sanctions to foster a culture of compliance within entities

The Act provides for a range of disciplinary and criminal sanctions for breaches of the Act. First, if the Commissioner ascertains that a lobbyist has gravely or repeatedly breached the obligations imposed on lobbyists by the Act or the Lobbyists Code of Conduct, the Commissioner may prohibit the registration of the lobbyist in the registry of lobbyists or order the cancellation of all entries in the registry concerning the lobbyist, for a maximum period of one year.

Second, a series of criminal sanctions may be applied depending on the nature of the offence. The Act's criminal sanctions regime makes it possible to punish certain acts, such as lobbying without being registered. The Act also provides for a number of other situations in which a lobbyist may be in violation, such as late registration or the inadvertent omission of certain information in the returns disclosed in the registry (Table 2.7). Lastly, since 2019, the Lobbying Act provides for a prescription period of five years from the date on which the Commissioner of Lobbying became aware of the offence to a maximum of ten years after the date of the commission of the offence. This development was sought by the Commissioner in Principle 27 of the Statement of Principles, proposing to establish a prescription regime adapted to the nature of the offences provided for by the Act and consistent with similar existing regimes in Québec (Principle 27 of the Statement of Principles).

Table 2.7. Criminal sanctions for breaches of the Act's obligations

Type of offence	Sanction
Contravening a registration provision or certain prohibitions prescribed by the Act	Fine of CAD 500 to CAD 25 000
Filing a return or notice in the Lobbyists Registry containing information that they know is false or misleading	Fine of CAD 500 to CAD 25 000
Hindering the action of the Commissioner or a person authorised by him/her in the exercise of an investigative power	Fine of CAD 500 to CAD 25 000
Violating a provision of the Lobbyists Code of Conduct	Fine of CAD 500 to CAD 25 000
Engaging in lobbying activities in contravention of a decision of the Lobbyists Commissioner prohibiting the registration of the lobbyist in the registry of lobbyists or ordering the cancellation of all entries in the registry concerning the lobbyist	Fine of CAD 500 to CAD 25 000

Source: (Légis Québec, 2002[10]).

The recommendation to implement disciplinary and criminal sanctions at the entity level, and not only at the individual level, to foster a culture of compliance within entities is a corollary of principles 9 and 10 proposed by the Commissioner of Lobbying, which aim to introduce into the law principles of good governance and monitoring of lobbying activities at the entity level, which would be held accountable for any failures of in-house lobbyists to lobby on their behalf.

The Act could give the Commissioner the power to impose administrative monetary penalties

Under the current Act, even if the Commissioner of Lobbying finds an administrative offence, he/she must still submit a report to the Director of Criminal and Penal Prosecutions. The Commissioner has expressed the wish to maintain penal and disciplinary penalties and introduce monetary administrative penalties that are proportional and adapted to the nature and seriousness of the offences, allowing for a sliding scale of penalties and their publication if deemed relevant for the purposes of the Act (Principle 25 of the Statement of Principles). The Commissioner had also expressed the wish to be granted the capacity, as part of disciplinary powers, to impose mandatory training on any interest representative (Proposal 26). Several parliamentary and municipal officials interviewed by the OECD supported the introduction of such an administrative sanctioning power for the Commissioner, as it would help to relieve the burden on the justice system and allow the nature of the sanction associated with an offence to be adjusted according to its seriousness or recidivism. Some Canadian lobbying jurisdictions provide for the imposition of administrative sanctions on lobbyists who fail to comply with their obligations.

Administrative monetary penalties also help to promote compliance and resolve cases of late submission or failure to register. Since the entry into force of the Lobbying Act in Ireland, the Standards in Public Office Commission has focused on encouraging compliance with the legislation through interactions with lobbyists to resolve any cases of non-compliance, including the issuance of fines for late reporting, before proceeding with further sanctions. The Commission concluded that increased communication and outreach to lobbyists early in the process reduced the number of cases involved in legal proceedings in 2018. The majority of lobbyists comply with their obligations when contacted by the investigation unit (Box 2.13).

> **Box 2.13. Financial penalties imposed by the Standards in Public Office Commission in Ireland**
>
> Part 4 of the Irish Regulation of Lobbying Act 2015 on enforcement provisions gives the Standards in Public Office Commission the authority to conduct investigations into possible contraventions to the Act, prosecute offences and issue fixed payment notices (FPN) of EUR 200 for late filing of lobbying returns.
>
> The Commission reviews all registrations to ensure that all persons who are required to register have done so and that they have registered correctly. The Commission can also request, by providing notice to a given registrant, further or corrected information when it considers that an application is incomplete, inaccurate or misleading.
>
> The Commission established a separate Complaints and Investigations Unit to manage investigations and prosecutions, and put in place procedures for investigating non-compliance in relation to unreported lobbying by both registered and non-registered persons, as well as non-compliance related to non-returns and late returns of lobbying activity:
>
> - Unregistered lobbying activity is monitored via open-source intelligence such as media articles, from the Register itself, or from complaints or other information received by the Commission;
> - Late returns by registered persons are monitored on the basis of information extracted from the lobbying register relating to the number of late returns and non-returns after each return deadline. The online register is designed to ensure that fixed payment notices are automatically issued to any person submitting a late return on lobbying activities. If the payment is not paid by the specified date, the Commission prosecutes the offence of submitting a late return.
>
> As observed in Commission annual reports, in most cases, compliance was achieved after receipt of the notice. In 2017, there were neither convictions nor investigations concluded, as this was the first year in which enforcement provisions were in effect. In 2018, 26 investigations were launched to gather evidence in relation to possible unreported or unregistered lobbying activity, of which 13 were discontinued (in part due to the person subsequently coming into compliance with the Act) and 13 remained ongoing at year's end.
>
> The Commission noted that the FPNs issued in respect of the three relevant periods of 2018 (270) were significantly lower than in 2017 (619), signalling a marked improvement in compliance with the deadlines.
>
> Source: (OECD, 2021[3]).

In France, the initial compliance and enforcement activities of the High Authority for transparency in public life have raised questions about the appropriateness of the sanctions provided for in the law. Interest representatives who fail to comply with their reporting obligations are subject to a criminal sanction of up to one year imprisonment and a fine of EUR 15 000. The sanction is similar for non-compliance with ethical obligations. The maximum amount of these fines is higher for legal persons. The HATVP concluded that the choice of criminal sanctions was not necessarily the most appropriate solution for punishing offences, due to the long and laborious procedures, and leading to a judgment that is probably perceived as light by the person concerned. It also concluded that the maximum fine for legal persons (EUR 75 000) is negligible for large companies. The scope of the penalty is further weakened by the difficulty of establishing the intentional element of the offence. The HATVP has recommended the implementation of a graduated system of administrative sanctions enabling it to provide a rapid and proportionate response through the application of direct financial sanctions (HATVP, 2021[17]).

The Act could allow certain information on breaches to be made public

In Principle 24 of its Statement of Principles, the Commissioner recommends that certain reports and recommendations or sanctions be made public where deemed relevant for the purposes of the Act. Indeed, the Quebec Act contains few provisions allowing the Commissioner to make public information regarding sanctions and deterring interest representatives who contravene the Act. With respect to disciplinary sanctions, the Commissioner is not authorised to disclose the nature of the offence that generated the sanction, which does not allow the citizen to know the fault and the reasons for the decision. With respect to criminal proceedings, where a person pleads guilty to a contravention of the Act before a court file is opened, this is not made public, which may serve the purpose of the offending lobbyists who can continue their activities without their breaches being made public.

Publication of certain decisions regarding violations does exist in other international jurisdictions such as France, as well as in other Canadian jurisdictions such as Alberta, Saskatchewan and British Columbia, and at the federal level. Oversight authorities must submit investigation reports to their respective legislatures. Ontario and the Yukon may also make public the identity of the person concerned and disclose the nature of the offence committed. The implementation of such provisions in these jurisdictions has shown that these mechanisms can be particularly effective in promoting compliance.

The Act could give the Commissioner of Lobbying more awareness-raising powers to ensure compliance

The OECD Recommendation encourages the implementation of mechanisms to raise awareness of expected rules and standards, to ensure a better understanding of the application of these rules and standards and to be able to deal effectively with reports of lobbying activities and complaints from the public (Principle 9 of the Recommendation). In its Statement of Principles, the Commissioner of Lobbying recommends strengthening the Commissioner's outreach powers, including:

- Set out the Commissioner's power to issue guidelines, orders and interpretive notices covering interpretation, application and compliance with the Act, as well as the power to exempt the publication of information related to lobbying activities if its disclosure may be prejudicial to an individual, entity or public institution (Principle 28 of the Statement of Principles).
- Introduce an educational mission specifically for the Commissioner of lobbying and the obligation to offer public institutions, interest representatives and citizens a program and tools for training and education on the regulatory framework established by the Act (Principle 30 of the Statement of Principles).
- Introduce a training program for elected officials and officers designated by public institutions, continuing education for external interest representatives and the responsibility for all registered entities to offer such training to their in-house interest representatives (Principle 31 of the Statement of Principles).

The stakeholders interviewed for this report confirmed the efforts already made by the Commissioner of Lobbying to make lobbyists aware of their obligations. For example, the Commissioner's customer service department offers general and specific training, ensures a regular presence at conventions and conferences, offers a set of guidelines on its website (explanatory and reference documents), and disseminates information via several newsletters (Lobbyscope and Info Registre Hebdo) (Table 2.8).

Table 2.8. Awareness actions carried out by the Quebec Commissioner of Lobbying

	Statistics 2019-2020	Statistics 2020-2021
Training courses offered (targeted and general fixed-date)	58	43
People met in the framework of these trainings (public officials, lobbyists and citizens)	2 347	1 068
Attendance at a congress	5	1
Articles published in specialised media	N/A	3
Advertising campaign	N/A	1
Recipients of the newsletter	9 413	9 509
Public institutions assisted in the drafting or updating of documents aimed at regulating the practice of lobbying	N/A	3
Press release	6	1
Subscribers to weekly mailings of new entries in the Lobbyists Registry (Info Registre Hebdo)	650	645
Visitors to the website	29 823	40 352
New subscribers to our Facebook, LinkedIn and Twitter accounts	N/A	121

Source: Information provided by the Quebec Commissioner of Lobbying.

The Commissioner's proposals appear to be consistent with the objective sought and meet a real need expressed by various stakeholders, including lobbyists subject to the Act. Such measures also exist in other jurisdictions. For example, the New York State Lobbying Act provides for a continuing education regime for all registered lobbyists (Box 2.14).

> **Box 2.14. Trainings for lobbyists in the State of New York**
>
> The New York State Joint Commission on Public Ethics (JCOPE), which administers the Lobbying Act, provides an online training course for individuals registered as lobbyists. Subject matter includes information provided in the Lobbying Act, the Public Officers Law, JCOPE regulations and advisory opinions, and the Election Law. The training also includes best practices for meeting the various statutory requirements.
>
> Each person registered as a lobbyist must complete this training course within 60 days of initial registration and at least once in any three-year period during which they are registered as a lobbyist.
>
> Source: New York State Joint Commission on Public Ethics, Ethics for Lobbyists Training, https://jcope.ny.gov/ethics-lobbyists-training

Enabling an effective review of the Act

The OECD Recommendation states that countries should review the functioning of their rules and guidelines related to lobbying on a periodic basis and make necessary adjustments in light of experience. This helps to identify strengths, but also gaps and implementation failures that need to be addressed to meet evolving public expectations for transparency in decision-making processes and to ensure that regulation takes into account the multiple ways in which interests can influence policy-making processes (Principle 10 of the Recommendation). From this perspective, it is important that any law or regulation on lobbying include a mechanism for periodic review.

The Act could include a periodic review mechanism to address new developments in lobbying

The regular review of established lobbying rules and guidelines, as well as their implementation and enforcement in practice, helps to strengthen the overall framework for lobbying and improve compliance. In Quebec, the review procedure set out in the Act provided for only one review five years after its coming into force. As such, the Commissioner proposes to establish a regular, mandatory process for the Act's revision as well as a submission and consultation mechanism allowing the Commissioner to formulate, in a timely manner, recommendations to a committee or any other appropriate authority under the jurisdiction of the National Assembly (Principle 34 of the Statement of Principles). The Quebec legislator could draw inspiration from the Irish legislation, which includes provisions for a regular review mechanism (Box 2.15).

Box 2.15. Review of the Lobbying Act in Ireland

Section 2 of the Lobbying Act provides for regular reviews of the operations of the Act. The first review of the Act took place in 2016. The report takes into account inputs received by key stakeholders, including persons carrying out lobbying activities and the bodies representing them. No recommendations were made by the government for amendments of the Lobbying Act. Subsequent reviews must take place every three years.

The first report found a high level of compliance with legislative requirements. Lobbyists highlighted the need for further education, guidance and assistance, which led the Commission to review its communication activities and guidance to lobbyists.

In its submission to the first review of the operation of the Act, the Commission recommended that any breaches of the cooling-off statutory provisions should be an offence under the Act. It also pointed to the lack of power to enforce the Act's post-employment provisions or to impose sanctions for persons who fail to comply with these provisions.

The Code of Conduct for persons carrying out lobbying activities, which came into effect on 1 January 2019, will also be reviewed every three years.

Source: (OECD, 2021[3]).

Proposals for action

In order to implement transparency of lobbying activities based on the relevance of the information declared, and to be as consistent as possible with international best practices, the OECD recommends that Quebec consider the following proposals.

Clarify registration and disclosure requirements for stakeholders

- The Act could clarify that timely registration should be a prerequisite for any lobbying activity.
- The Act could reduce and harmonise registration deadlines for all lobbyists.
- The registry should place the obligation to register on entities, not individuals, while including the identity of each lobbyist.
- The Act could give entities the possibility to assume responsibility for reporting the lobbying activities of their member entities.
- The registration of non-profit organisations should not include the names of volunteers engaged in lobbying activities.

Strengthening the content of the information declared in the registry

- The Quebec legislator could take into account the expectations of the various stakeholders in order to delimit a relevant disclosure regime.
- The reporting requirements only imperfectly meet the transparency objectives of the Act and would benefit from being clarified to include the objective pursued and the specific decision targeted.
- The Act could provide for monitoring of activities by implementing regular disclosure to ensure timely access to lobbying information.

Maximising the technological environment of the Lobbyists Registry as a vehicle for transparency and accountability

- The Commissioner could maximise the use of the new platform to make the practical reality of lobbying more visible.
- The registry could include incentive mechanisms such as automatic reminders to lobbyists about disclosure obligations.
- The implementation of automatic verifications by the Commissioner could be useful to foster public scrutiny.

Sharing the responsibility of transparency with public decision-makers

- The Quebec legislator could consider implementing open agenda initiatives for certain public officials.
- Disclosure of the normative footprint could also complement the information contained in the Lobbyists Registry.

Implement mechanisms for effective enforcement and compliance with disclosure obligations

- The Quebec legislator should ensure that the Commissioner of Lobbying has sufficient powers to carry out his duties.

- The Act could implement sanctions at the entity level to foster a culture of compliance within entities.
- The Act could give the Commissioner of Lobbying the power to impose administrative monetary penalties.
- The Act could allow certain information on breaches to be made public
- The Act could give the Commissioner of Lobbying more educational powers to ensure compliance.

Enabling an effective review of the Lobbying Act

- The Act could include a periodic review mechanism to respond to changes in lobbying.

References

Ceres (2021), *Shareholders approve a climate lobbying proposal at Delta, continuing a winning streak that shows the importance of Paris-aligned climate policy*, https://www.ceres.org/news-center/press-releases/shareholders-approve-climate-lobbying-proposal-delta-continuing-winning. [7]

Glass Lewis (2021), *2020 Proxy Season Review*, https://glasslewis.com/wp-content/uploads/2021/09/Shareholder-Proposals-2021-Proxy-Season-Review.pdf. [9]

HATVP (2021), *L'encadrement de la représentation d'intérêts. Bilan, enjeux de l'extension du répertoire à l'échelon local et propositions*, https://www.hatvp.fr/wordpress/wp-content/uploads/2021/11/HATVP_Rapport_lobbying_web_2021-VF.pdf. [17]

Légis Québec (2002), *Lobbying Transparency and Ethics Act*, https://www.legisquebec.gouv.qc.ca/en/document/cs/T-11.011. [10]

Lobbyisme Québec (2021), *Consultation sur les modalités entourant les déclarations à la future plateforme de divulgation des activités de lobbyisme*, https://lobbyisme.quebec/salledepresse/consultation-sur-les-modalites-entourant-les-declarations-a-la-future-plateforme-de-divulgation-des-activites-de-lobbyisme/?tx_news_pi1%5Bcontroller%5D=News&tx_news_pi1%5Baction%5D=detail&cHash=4c50ea7b5cd2e2eb6d6581. [15]

Lobbyisme Québec (2019), *Projet de modalités de tenue du registre des lobbyistes*, https://lobbyisme.quebec/fileadmin/Centre_de_documentation/Documentation_institutionnelle/projet-modalites-tenue-registre-lobbyistes.pdf. [6]

Lobbyisme Québec (2019), *Simplicité, Clarté, Pertinence, Efficacité. Réforme de l'encadrement du lobbyisme*, https://www.commissairelobby.qc.ca/fileadmin/Centre_de_documentation/Documentation_institutionnelle/2019-06-13_Enonce-principes-CLQ.pdf. [14]

Lobbyisme Québec (2017), *La révision de la loi sur la transparence et l'éthique en matière de lobbyisme. Le temps est à l'action. Amendements proposés au projet de loi no 56*, https://www.commissairelobby.qc.ca/fileadmin/user_upload/128_presentation_des_amendements_au_projet_de_loi_no_56.pdf. [13]

Lobbyisme Québec (2012), *Avis 2012-01 du Commissaire. L'objet des activités de lobbyismes, les institutions publiques visées et la période couverte par les activités*, https://lobbyisme.quebec/wp-content/uploads/2021/07/Avis_2012_01.pdf. [11]

Lobbyisme Québec (n.d.), *Comité consultatif de Lobbyisme Québec*, https://lobbyisme.quebec/a-propos/organisation/comite-consultatif-du-commissaire-au-lobbyisme-du-quebec/#:~:text=Ce%20comit%C3%A9%20vise%20%C3%A0%20faire,et%20du%20commissaire%20au%20lobbyisme. [16]

OECD (2021), *Lobbying in the 21st Century: Transparency, Integrity and Access*, OECD Publishing, Paris, https://doi.org/10.1787/c6d8eff8-en. [3]

OECD (2017), *Recommendation of the Council on Open Government*, https://legalinstruments.oecd.org/en/instruments/OECD-LEGAL-0438. [1]

OECD (2014), *Lobbyists, Governments and Public Trust, Volume 3: Implementing the OECD Principles for Transparency and Integrity in Lobbying*, OECD Publishing, Paris, https://doi.org/10.1787/9789264214224-en. [4]

OECD (2010), *OECD Recommendation on Principles for Transparency and Integrity in Lobbying*, https://www.oecd.org/corruption/ethics/Lobbying-Brochure.pdf. [2]

Office of the Commissioner of Lobbying of Canada (2021), *Improving the Lobbying Act. Preliminary Recommendations. Provided in response to a request from the House of Commons Standing Committee on Access to Information, Privacy and Ethics*, https://lobbycanada.gc.ca/media/1933/leg-improving-the-lobbying-act-submission-preliminary-recommendations-2021-02-12-en.pdf. [5]

Office of the Commissioner of Lobbying of Canada (2020), *Annual Report 2019-20*, https://lobbycanada.gc.ca/en/reports-and-publications/annual-report-2019-20/. [12]

Principles for Responsible Investment (2018), *Converging on Climate Lobbying. Aligning Corporate Practice Within Investor Expectations*, https://www.unpri.org/Uploads/g/v/q/PRI_Converging_on_climate_lobbying.pdf. [8]

Note

[3] These lobbyists include lobbyists working in companies, consulting firms and NGOs.

3 Promote a culture of integrity in the interactions between public officials and lobbyists in Quebec

This chapter reviews the Quebec integrity framework from the perspective of interactions between public officials (public office holders) and lobbyists. On the one hand, the integrity framework for public officials offers the opportunity to complement the Lobbying Transparency and Ethics Act. To this end, the chapter provides recommendations on how the integrity framework could be clarified and strengthened with regard to the obligations of public officials. In addition, the chapter discusses the Lobbyists' Code of Conduct as a starting point for promoting responsible engagement.

Introduction

Reforming the legislative framework (Chapter 1) and improving transparency to allow for better public scrutiny of the policy-making process (Chapter 2) are key elements in regulating lobbying and addressing the risks of undue influence and inequity in the power to influence.

Beyond these reforms, it is imperative to promote a culture of integrity in the interactions between public officials and lobbyists more broadly, and to have a strategic view of the system. Indeed, laws and regulations will always be incomplete and will never be able to cover all the grey areas and practices of influence, however well they are designed. Hence the importance of seeing the interactions between interest representatives and public officials also as a field of applied ethics, where common sense and the internal ethical compass must play a role on both sides.

The OECD Recommendation on Principles for Transparency and Integrity in Lobbying states that countries should foster a culture of integrity in public organisations and decision making by providing clear rules and guidelines of conduct for public officials (Principle 7 of the Recommendation). The Recommendation also states lobbyists should comply with standards of professionalism and transparency; they share responsibility for fostering a culture of transparency and integrity in lobbying (Principle 8 of the Recommendation).

This requires, on the one hand, the establishment of clear rules and guidelines of conduct for public officials. On the other hand, lobbyists themselves can help to ensure the integrity of their engagement with public officials through self-regulatory mechanisms, such as a code of conduct and a monitoring and enforcement system.

Strengthening the integrity framework for public officials

The OECD Recommendation calls on countries to foster a culture of integrity in public bodies and in public decision-making by establishing clear rules and guidelines governing the behaviour of public officials. Specifically, the Recommendation states that countries should provide principles, rules, standards and procedures that give public officials clear directions on how they are permitted to engage with lobbyists. Public officials should conduct their communication with lobbyists in line with relevant rules, standards and guidelines in a way that bears the closest public scrutiny. In particular, they should cast no doubt on their impartiality to promote the public interest, share only authorised information and not misuse 'confidential information', disclose relevant private interests and avoid conflict of interest. Decision makers should also set an example by their personal conduct in their relationship with lobbyists.

Quebec could therefore strengthen the current integrity framework by considering the following measures that will be detailed in the following sections:

- Clarify and, if necessary, establish or strengthen specific integrity standards for public officials and the behaviour expected vis-à-vis lobbying activities.
- Intensify awareness raising and training of public officials on the standards, challenges and risks of lobbying, in particular by including the topic more explicitly in ethics training, especially at the municipal level.
- Give ethics advisors the responsibility and ability to respond to public officials' doubts about the law and the risks of lobbying practices.

The following recommendations will also highlight the importance of coordination between the Quebec Commissioner of Lobbying, the Treasury Board Secretariat (TBS), the Ethics Commissioner of the National Assembly and the Quebec Municipal Commission. Although these bodies are already in contact and share information, the institutionalisation of a regular coordination mechanism between them could contribute to a more strategic vision of the challenges related to lobbying and ensure lasting constructive cooperation and coordination, as well as allow for the development of joint initiatives and make the link with other initiatives aimed at improving transparency and integrity more explicit, such as, for example, Quebec's 2021-2023 Action Plan for Open Government.

Clarify and, if necessary, establish or strengthen specific integrity standards for public officials and the behaviour expected from lobbying activities

In an age of social media and information overload, and where back and forth between the private and public sectors is commonplace, public officials are constantly exposed to public scrutiny and criticism, risking the collapse of their reputations every time an intervention is misperceived or misinterpreted. Public officials therefore need more than ever an integrity framework adapted to the specific risks of lobbying and other influence practices. While rules on conflict of interest management, gifts, entertainment and meals are strong, standards, guidelines and capacity building specific to lobbying and other influence practices can be improved.

Despite the guidance of the OECD Recommendation, only a few countries have developed specific standards for public officials regarding their interactions with lobbyists (Figure 3.1). At the federal level, Canada is among the countries that have included standards in this regard, notably in the Prime Minister's Guide to Open and Accountable Government for Ministers and Ministers of State (Premier ministre du Canada, 2015[1]). The Guide clearly links fundraising activities and dealings with lobbyists with the obligation of Ministers and Parliamentary Secretaries to avoid any conflict of interest, any appearance of conflict of interest and any situation that could give rise to a conflict of interest (Annex B of the Guide, see also Box 3.1 below). Also, the Conflict of Interest Code for Members of the House of Commons and the Conflict of Interest and Ethics Code for Senators state that Members of the House of Commons and Senators may not use their office to influence the decision of another person in a way that favours his or her own personal interests or those of a member of his or her family or, in an improper manner, those of any other person or entity.

Figure 3.1. More standards are needed for public officials on their interactions with lobbyists

Specific duties and standards of conduct related to lobbying activities for public officials

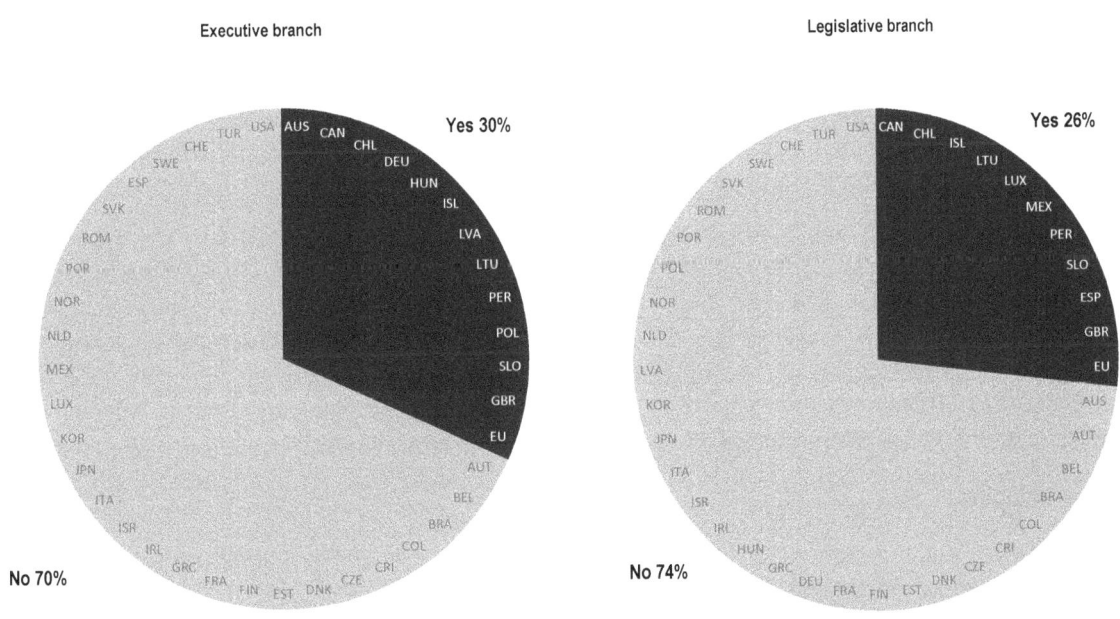

Source: (OECD, 2021[2]).

Depending on the type of document in which the standards are included, standards for public officials and their interactions with lobbyists may include, for example (OECD, 2021[2]):

- The duty to treat lobbyists equally by granting them fair and equal access.
- The obligation to refuse meetings with unregistered lobbyists.
- The obligation to report violations to the competent authorities.
- The obligation to register their meetings with lobbyists (see Chapter 2 on public agendas).

In Quebec, the Lobbying Transparency and Ethics Act was adopted to provide a framework for lobbying activities and make them more transparent. This Act therefore applies mainly to lobbyists, not to public officials. Nevertheless, it is important to clarify the obligations and expectations regarding the behaviour of public officials who may be targeted by influence initiatives.

In addition, the *Regulation respecting ethics and discipline in the public service* and the *Declaration of values of the Quebec public administration* consolidate the rules of ethics and reaffirm the fundamental values of ethics. For members of the National Assembly, the *Code of Ethics and Conduct* applies; it also extends to ministers and political staff. For municipalities, there is the *Municipal Ethics and Good Conduct Act*. However, these ethical guidelines do not contain explicit references to the expected and desired conduct of public officials with regard to lobbying. Only the Code of Ethics and Conduct for Members of the National Assembly stipulates that a Member may not engage in lobbying activities within the meaning of the Lobbying Transparency and Ethics Act.

The Quebec Commissioner of Lobbying, in coordination with the Treasury Board Secretariat, the Ethics Commissioner of the National Assembly and the Quebec Municipal Commission, could develop awareness-raising material such as brochures or guides for public officials on standards and good practices. Annex B of the Prime Minister's Guide to Open and Accountable Government for Ministers and Ministers of State of the Canadian federal government could serve as inspiration and a basis for developing this kind of guidance (Box 3.1).

Box 3.1. Fundraising and Dealing with Lobbyists: Best Practices for Ministers and Parliamentary Secretaries in the Prime Minister's Guide to Open and Accountable Government (excerpt)

Appendix B of the Canadian federal government's Guide to Open and Accountable Government summarises the best practices that Ministers and Parliamentary Secretaries should follow to maintain appropriate boundaries between their official duties and political fundraising activities. It is important that Ministers and Parliamentary Secretaries familiarize themselves with these practices and apply them in all appropriate circumstances. In addition, they must ensure that their staffs are well acquainted with the practices and that adequate processes are in place in their offices to ensure compliance.

The practices complement, and do not replace, other rules that Ministers and Parliamentary Secretaries must observe, including the *Conflict of Interest Act*, the *Conflict of Interest Code for Members of the House of Commons* and the *Lobbying Act*. Ministers and Parliamentary Secretaries should communicate with the Office of the Conflict of Interest and Ethics Commissioner if they have any questions or concerns relating to their obligations under the *Conflict of Interest Act* or the *Conflict of Interest Code for Members of the House of Commons*, and should familiarize themselves with the Commissioner's *Guidelines on Fundraising and the Conflict of Interest Act*.

General principles

- Ministers and Parliamentary Secretaries must ensure that political fundraising activities or considerations do not affect, or appear to affect, the exercise of their official duties or the access of individuals or organizations to government.

- There should be no preferential access to government, or appearance of preferential access, accorded to individuals or organizations because they have made financial contributions to politicians and political parties.
- There should be no singling out, or appearance of singling out, of individuals or organizations as targets of political fundraising because they have official dealings with Ministers and Parliamentary Secretaries, or their staff or departments.

Departmental Stakeholders

In this document, "departmental stakeholders" includes:

- Lobbyists registered to lobby Ministers and Parliamentary Secretaries, their staff or their departments;
- Employees of lobbying firms retained to lobby Ministers, Parliamentary Secretaries, their staff or their departments;
- Employees of corporations and organizations whose employees are registered to lobby Ministers, Parliamentary Secretaries, their staff or their departments; and
- Individuals employed in, contracted by, or who otherwise represent corporations and organizations that have current or anticipated official dealings with Ministers, Parliamentary Secretaries, their staff or their departments.

Specific best practices

In order to ensure that there is no differential treatment or appearance of differential treatment for individuals, corporations or organizations because of their financial support of politicians or political parties, Ministers and Parliamentary Secretaries should adopt the following best practices:

- Ministers and Parliamentary Secretaries should not seek to have departmental stakeholders included on fundraising or campaign teams or on the boards of electoral district associations.
- Ministers and Parliamentary Secretaries should establish and maintain appropriate safeguards to ensure that lists and contact or other identifying information of departmental stakeholders are not provided to those engaged in fundraising activities.
- Ministers and Parliamentary Secretaries should ensure that government facilities and equipment, including ministerial or departmental letterhead, are not used for or in connection with fundraising activities.
- Ministers and Parliamentary Secretaries should ensure that the solicitation of political contributions on their behalf does not target: departmental stakeholders, or other lobbyists and employees of lobbying firms (note that this is not intended to restrict general fundraising appeals made to a broad group of supporters or potential supporters).
- Ministers, Parliamentary Secretaries and their staff should not discuss departmental business at any fundraising event, and should refer any person who wishes to discuss departmental business to make an appointment with the Minister's office or department as appropriate.
- Ministers and Parliamentary Secretaries should ensure that fundraising communications issued on their behalf do not suggest any connection between fundraising and official government business.
- Ministers, Parliamentary Secretaries and their staff should exercise caution in meeting with consultant lobbyists, and should give particular consideration to whether it is appropriate to meet a consultant lobbyist in the absence of the lobbyist's client.

Source: https://pm.gc.ca/en/news/backgrounders/2015/11/27/open-and-accountable-government#Lobbyists

In addition, the Quebec legislator could consider strengthening the duties and obligations regarding the behaviour expected of public officials. In particular, Quebec could consider clarifying the responsibility of public officials to enforce the Lobbying Transparency and Ethics Act and strengthen the regulation of the "revolving door".

Clarify the responsibility of public officials to enforce the Lobbying Transparency and Ethics Act

At present, the Lobbying Transparency and Ethics Act does not clearly assign responsibilities to the State, public institutions and public office holders with regard to the transparency of lobbying activities. This responsibility is mentioned only in passing in section 1 by the affirmation of the right of citizens to be informed of influence communications made to public institutions. In particular, the Act does not clearly confer a responsibility on public officials to ensure that those who attempt to influence them are registered in the Lobbyists Registry.

The Quebec Commissioner of Lobbying's Diagnostic already highlighted the reluctance and criticism of certain elected officials and staff of public institutions with respect to the Act, going so far as to reject any form of responsibility that might fall to them to ensure compliance with the Act (Lobbyisme Québec, 2019[3]). The consultations conducted by the Commissioner of Lobbying in 2018 revealed that many elected officials and civil servants still do not feel responsible for ensuring compliance with the Act. The consultations conducted by the OECD confirm this feeling. Moreover, several parliamentary and municipal elected officials interviewed disagree with the idea that the Act gives them a formal responsibility to ensure compliance. While some of them fear that these obligations will hamper citizens' access to elected officials, others say they fear the multiplication of legal requirements and social pressures, for example on the position of MP or mayor.

While public officials effectively cannot and should not play the role of monitoring the application of the Act in general, it seems conceivable to require a degree of responsibility on the part of public officials to ensure that those who contact them are indeed registered as lobbyists or are covered by exemptions (Chapter 1). This due diligence on the part of public officials should be clearly specified in the expected standards of conduct and of course requires enhanced awareness raising, training and guidance for public officials. For example, EU Commissioners and members of their cabinets must refuse to meet with non-registered lobbyists. In Slovenia, public officials can only agree to enter into contact with a lobbyist after verifying that the lobbyist is registered.

In this regard, the Treasury Board Secretariat suggests in its various directives on contract management that departments and public bodies obtain a declaration from the contractor that he or she complies with the provisions of the Lobbying Transparency and Ethics Act before awarding any contract. In addition, several municipalities, ministries or public agencies have adopted various policies in recent years requiring their staff members to ensure that the lobbyists they meet are duly registered in the Lobbyists Registry.

At a minimum, the various codes of conduct applicable to public office holders could, for example, include guidelines and remind public officials of the need to be vigilant about influence communications. In the Netherlands, for example, the Code of Conduct on Integrity in Central Government reminds public officials of the need to take into account the indirect ways in which they can be influenced by special interest groups, such as through research funding (Box 3.2).

> **Box 3.2. Netherlands: the Code of Conduct on Integrity in Central Government reminds public officials to pay attention to indirect influence**
>
> "You may have to deal with lobbyists in your work. These are advocates who try to influence decision making to their advantage. That is allowed. But are you always aware of that? And how do you deal with it?
>
> Make sure you can do your work transparently and independently. Be aware of the interests of lobbyists and of the different possibilities of influence. This can be done very directly (for example by a visit or invitation), but also more indirectly (for example by co-financing research that influences policy).
>
> Consult with your colleagues or supervisor where these situations may be present in your work.
>
> Sometimes it is in the public interest to avoid contacts with lobbyists".
>
> Source: Extracts from the Dutch Code of Conduct on Integrity in Central Government, https://zoek.officielebekendmakingen.nl/stcrt-2019-71141.html.

Strengthening the rules before, during and after a public mandate

Revolving doors occur when public officials migrate to areas of activity for which they were responsible, or when professionals from these areas become public office holders. Often these changes are accompanied by the possibility of exploiting the networks of influence of these people, including access to privileged information or individuals, in the case of 'outgoing' public officials (Yates, 2018[4]). These former public officials can therefore be coveted as future lobbyists and monetise their networks and information on the public sector. Yet, empirical analysis shows that public officials coming from the private sector can lead to similar problems (Faccio, 2006[5]) .

In Quebec, the Act does not formally prohibit elected municipal officials and employees of public institutions from also being lobbyists during or after their public mandate. While the Act includes formal prohibitions for ministers, members of the executive council and their close advisors when they leave public office (sections 28 and 29 of the Act), only the Code of Ethics and Conduct for Members of the National Assembly goes further by covering lobbying activities carried out while in public office. This code stipulates that a Member may not engage in lobbying activities within the meaning of the Lobbying Transparency and Ethics Act. The Commissioner calls for a the establishment of disclosure and confidentiality obligations, an ethical framework and specific prohibitions applicable to lobbying activities undertaken by elected officials or officers designated by public institutions during and after the end of their term or duties for the public institutions with which they had or maintained connections or official relations (Principle 15 of the Statement of Principles). These rules generally consist of a cooling-off period during which a former public official may not engage in lobbying activities with bodies where he or she previously held a job or office or with which he or she had privileged contacts. A waiver power, granted to the Commissioner, would aim to meet this need for flexibility in exceptional circumstances. Such a power already exists in many jurisdictions.

Canadian federal law, which is stricter than Quebec law in this regard, imposes a five-year prohibition on lobbying activities by designated public office holders after they leave office. These rules are, however, limited to designated office holders within the meaning of the Act, i.e. those who hold the highest responsibilities in public institutions.

Second, the Commissioner also recommended that the framework must also allow the Commissioner of lobbying to grant a full or partial exemption from such obligations, rules or prohibitions when doing so is not contrary to the spirit of the Act (Principle 15 of the Statement of Principles). Such measures exist, for example, at the European Union level (Box 3.3).

> ### Box 3.3. Post-employment rules at the EU level
>
> **Members of the European Commission**
>
> The Code of Conduct for Members of the European Commission establishes a two-year "scrutiny period" (three years for the former Commission President) during which Commissioners must notify the professional activities in which they intend to engage during this period. If the intended activity is linked to the Commissioner's former portfolio, the Commission must first consult an Independent Ethical Committee before approving the activities.
>
> **European civil service**
>
> Members of the EU civil service leaving their position and beginning a new job within two years must obtain authorisation from the relevant institution. If the activity is related to work carried out during their last three years in service and might conflict with the legitimate interests of the institution, the institution may forbid it or approve it subject to conditions.
>
> Senior officials (Directors General and Directors) are prohibited, in the twelve months after leaving service, from engaging in lobbying activities targeting their former institutions on matters for which they were responsible during their last three years in service.
>
> Source: Code of Conduct for Members of the European Union; Code of Conduct for Members of the European Parliament; Staff regulations for Members of the European civil service.

As regards the other direction of the revolving doors, rules requiring former lobbyists who have become public office holders not to deal in their new positions with issues similar to those they dealt with as lobbyists are rather rare. However, some countries and states in the United States impose such a time limit on the election, appointment or hiring of an interest representative as a public office holder. In the United States, Maryland law, as an exception, also imposes a one-year ban on any lobbyist becoming a public office holder before he or she can act on matters on which he or she has previously worked as a lobbyist. In France, restrictions also apply before public employment (Box 3.4).

> ### Box 3.4. Post and pre-public employment restrictions in France
>
> **Post-employment restrictions**
>
> - For a period of three years, former ministers, presidents of local executives and members of an independent administrative authority must refer to the HATVP to examine whether the new private activities they plan to pursue are compatible with their former functions.
>
> - Public bodies also control the transition of former public servants to the private sector, which is carried out by the hierarchical superior of the civil servant concerned. The hierarchical superior may refer individual cases to the HATVP in case of doubt. Referral to the HATVP is mandatory for certain senior civil servants.
>
> **Pre-employment restrictions**
>
> France, article 432 of the Penal Code imposes certain restrictions on private-sector employees hired to fill a post in a public administration. For a period of three years following the termination of their functions in their previous employment, they must not be entrusted with the supervision or control of a private undertaking, with the conclusion of contracts of any kind with a private undertaking or with giving an

opinion on such contracts. They are also not allowed to propose decisions relating to the operations carried out by a private undertaking or formulate opinions on such decisions. They must not receive advice from or any capital in one of these undertakings. Any breach to this provision is punished by two years' imprisonment and a fine of EUR 30 000.

In 2020, the HATVP was entrusted with a new 'pre-appointment' check for certain senior positions. A preventive check is carried out before an appointment to certain high-level positions (notably members of a ministerial cabinet, aides to the President of the Republic, directors of central administration), if a person has held a position in the private sector in the three years preceding the appointment.

Source: (OECD, 2021[2])

Increase awareness and training of public officials on the standards, challenges and risks of lobbying, in particular by including the subject more explicitly in ethics training, especially at municipal level

Beyond clarifying and establishing standards of conduct, responsibilities and obligations, it is essential to ensure that these standards are effectively translated into the daily practice of public officials. Laws and codes of conduct or ethics are the necessary basis, but are not sufficient to achieve this goal. In addition, the standards should be communicated in a simple and clear manner and public officials need to understand the rationale behind the regulations, be aware of the risks and know how to apply the guidelines in their daily work.

In Quebec, despite the fact that the obligation to comply with the law rests with lobbyists, the Commissioner's training and awareness activities are also directed at the public sector, although little training is conducted at the municipal level. At the same time, the increased co-responsibility recommended in this report also requires that public officials be adequately prepared and accompanied. Moreover, the Commissioner provides information material and training guides on its website for parliamentary, government and municipal office holders.

Nevertheless, to date, despite the material made available by the Commissioner and the fact that the subject of lobbying is part of the basic ethics training, the OECD consultations established that this aspect could and certainly should be strengthened. Indeed, the rules on lobbying and their relation to the integrity framework are not well known. Indeed, the officials consulted by the OECD perceive a certain level of ignorance within the public administration about lobbying, its concept, its practices and the ethical implications that interactions between the public sector and lobbyists bring with them. In a 2018 survey of elected officials and staff of public institutions, only one in two respondents (52%) considered themselves sufficiently informed about the rules governing lobbying in their workplace (Lobbyisme Québec, 2019[3]). Also, there is reason to assume that in general, and similar to citizens' perceptions, lobbying is perceived by officials as an activity with a negative connotation.

This need for training is particularly visible at the municipal level, where the density and continuity of relations between citizens, local actors and public officials create grey areas and where the heterogeneity of the local and municipal environment makes the challenges perhaps even greater. Indeed, in consultations conducted by the OECD, municipal representatives expressed a desire for more training and guidance on the subject of lobbying.

In its Statement of Principles, the Commissioner recommends introducing a training regime for elected officials and designated officers of public institutions (Principle 31 of the Statement of Principles). Increased coordination between the Quebec Commissioner of Lobbying, the Treasury Board Secretariat, the Ethics Commissioner of the National Assembly and the Quebec Municipal Commission in the area of lobbying and integrity could allow for the strengthening of awareness and training activities on the integrity standards applicable to public officials in the specific context of lobbying activities. In this regard, the Commissioner has proposed on several occasions to integrate specific terms and conditions into the laws aimed at municipalities, by tabling briefs in committees, in particular to ensure that the framework remains concentrated in the Act and consistent across all levels (Lobbyisme Québec, 2009[6]; 2010[7]; 2021[8]). In Ireland, for example, the Public Service Standards Commission provides tailored guidance to various categories of public officials to promote awareness and understanding is incorporated into the Lobbying Act (Box 3.5).

The Quebec Commissioner of Lobbying recommends to introduce an educational mission specifically for the Commissioner of lobbying and the obligation to offer public institutions, interest representatives and citizens a program and tools for training and education on the regulatory framework established by the Act (Principle 30 of the Statement of Principles). In particular, Quebec could therefore increase its efforts to raise awareness and train public officials. This may require expanding the Quebec Commissioner of Lobbying's mandate to include education and communication to public officials, while ensuring close coordination with other relevant bodies to maximise synergies and align messages.

- **Awareness raising**: It is important that public officials are aware of the rationale behind the legal provisions and the conduct expected of them. Knowing why it is important to promote transparency and integrity in relations with interest representatives, knowing the risks associated with it, as well as knowing how to recognise the different direct and indirect practices of influence is essential to bring about a change in conduct. In addition to providing information material as recommended above, the Quebec Commissioner of Lobbying, in coordination with the Treasury Board Secretariat, the Ethics Commissioner of the National Assembly and the Quebec Municipal Commission, could initiate campaigns to communicate more actively with public officials. Increased collaboration could also be implemented with representative organisations such as the Union des municipalités du Québec (UMQ) or the Fédération québécoise des municipalités (FQM), which offer training programmes addressing the issue of lobbying for elected municipal officials.

- **Training:** Despite its importance, training specifically on integrity in interactions with lobbyists is rare. Among legislators surveyed by the OECD in 38 jurisdictions, 64% said they had not received training or information on how to interact with lobbyists (OECD, 2021[1]). Most of the countries surveyed offer training and awareness-raising activities on specific issues, such as integrity in interactions with third parties on an ad hoc basis. The tailor-made training by videoconference for public departments and agencies proposed by the Commissioner in Quebec is certainly a good practice to pursue. In addition, Quebec could consider including the relationship with interest representatives more intensively in the ethics training offered at the level of the public service, the National Assembly or, in the case of municipalities, by the Union des municipalités du Québec (UMC) or the Fédération québécoise des municipalités (FQM). Case studies on lobbying, based on real cases, could enable public officials to understand the concepts, risks and practices so that they can make better decisions to protect the public interest and themselves. In addition, training could in particular address the new challenges of indirect lobbying and help public officials to assess the reliability of information received. The training guides for parliamentary, governmental and municipal office holders provided by the Commissioner of Lobbying could be updated and inform training.

> **Box 3.5. Tailor-made advice for public officials in Ireland**
>
> In Ireland, section 17 of the Lobbying Act states that "the Commission may issue guidance on the operation of this Act and may from time to time revise or republish it", and "may make available specific information to promote awareness and understanding of this Act".
>
> The website www.lobbying.ie contains specific guidance for public officials covered by the provisions of the Act ("designated public officials"), including:
>
> - General guidance for public officials to ensure that they understand how the system works, how they fit into it and how they can help support the implementation of the legislation.
> - Advice to members of the Dáil, members of the Seanad and members of the European Parliament representing the Irish Government.
> - Advice to members of local authorities.
> - Advice on the reflection period.
>
> Source: (OECD, 2021[2]); https://www.lobbying.ie/help-resources/information-for-dpos/.

Build the capacity of ethical advisors to prepare them to respond to questions from public officials about the Act and the risks associated with lobbying practices

Standards and norms of conduct need to be communicated simply and clearly, and the government needs to invest in awareness-raising campaigns and training to build the capacity necessary for effective understanding and application of the law. In addition, international experience with ethical enforcement shows that it is essential to provide a known and easily accessible institutional support function for public official (OECD, 2020[9]; OECD, 2009[10]). They need to have a trusted person or unit to turn to in case of specific doubt.

This advice and consultation is provided by dedicated integrity committees, units or staff. The integrity advisory function can take different forms: within a central government body, through an independent or semi-independent specialised body; or through integrity units or advisors within ministries or the legislature or judiciary. Their role is usually to provide advice on resolving ethical dilemmas and to help public officials understand public ethics rules and principles. These approaches generally cover standards of conduct and public service values, but they could still improve understanding and knowledge of the risks associated with lobbying and the behaviour expected of public officials. In those countries that have developed specific integrity standards for lobbying, the majority also provide advice on how to apply the regulations and guidelines. Assistance may be available online, or by calling a specific hotline or emailing a dedicated contact.

At the level of the legislature, the majority of countries responding to the OECD survey reported having an integrity function within their organisation or a specialised institution to guide their interactions with lobbyists (OECD, 2021[2]). In France, for example, the High Authority for the Transparency of Public Life (HATVP) provides individual confidential advice on request to the highest elected and non-elected public officials within its scope, and provides guidance and support to their institution when requested by one of these public officials, within 30 days of receiving the request (OECD, 2020[9]).

In Quebec, the Network of ethical advisors (*Réseau des répondants en éthique de la fonction publique Québécoise*), set up in 2002 by the Treasury Board Secretariat, aims to support the work of ethics officers in their respective departments and agencies. Each department appoints at least one ethics officer/advisor. At the municipal level, the Quebec Municipal Commission publishes a list of municipal ethics advisors who can answer any questions elected officials may have about their codes of ethics. For members of the National Assembly, the Ethics Commissioner is an independent institution responsible for ensuring compliance with the ethical principles and application of the rules of conduct that must guide the conduct of members of the Assembly and their staff.

Although a detailed analysis of this ethical framework in the Québec public service is not the subject of this study, the consultations conducted by the OECD revealed a certain disparity between departments in terms of the resources invested in ethics. Also, the function of ethics officer is normally added to the functions already under the responsibility of the public official, thus limiting the time that the public official can dedicate to the promotion of public integrity within his or her organisation.

The OECD consultations also showed that at present there is a lack of clarity among civil servants about where to seek advice regarding interaction with interest representatives. The ethics officers consulted responded that they are already sometimes consulted on the subject; if in doubt, they refer the request to the Commissioner of Lobbying. A good practice in Quebec, which could inspire other organisations, is found in the Ministry of Transport, which has developed an internal directive on lobbying, has established mandatory training and has included lobbying in its risk management and integrity plans. In addition, they mentor civil servants who are approached by lobbyists.

Once again, the Quebec Commissioner of Lobbying, the Treasury Board Secretariat, the Ethics Commissioner of the National Assembly and the Quebec Municipal Commissioner could combine their efforts and align their messages in order to prepare ethics officers to respond to doubts related to lobbying, to guide and advise them and, if necessary, to coach or even accompany public servants during their interactions with interest representatives. This recommendation is partly consistent with that made by the Quebec Commissioner of Lobbying in its Statement of Principles, where it is recommended to designate the primary officer of any public institution or any person within that institution to whom the officer will delegate the responsibility as reference person for the application of and compliance with the Act within the institution (Principle 14 of the Statement of Principles). This responsibility could be given to the Ethics Officer. This person would be responsible for ensuring that the objectives of the law are met and that it is respected within the institution.

As a second line of defence, the Quebec Commissioner of Lobbying, the Treasury Board Secretariat, the Ethics Commissioner of the National Assembly and the Quebec Municipal Commissioner should continue to be available to support these respondents and ethics advisors in case of doubt or to arbitrate grey areas.

Promoting responsible engagement of lobbyists

Companies and organisations are also increasingly exposed to public scrutiny. Lobbyists acting on their behalf therefore need a clear integrity framework when intervening in the public policy process. The OECD Recommendation recalls that governments and legislators have the primary responsibility for establishing clear standards of conduct for public officials who are lobbied. However, lobbyists and their clients, as the ordering party, also bear an obligation to ensure that they avoid exercising illicit influence and comply with professional standards in their relations with public officials, with other lobbyists and their clients, and with the public (Principle 8 of the Recommendation). In addition, to maintain trust in public decision making, in-house and consultant lobbyists should also promote principles of good governance. In particular, they should conduct their contact with public officials with integrity and honesty, provide reliable and accurate information, and avoid conflict of interest in relation to both public officials and the clients they represent, for example by not representing conflicting or competing interests (Principle 8 of the Recommendation).

At the OECD level, codes of conduct instituted at the level of companies, organisations or their groupings, continue to be the main tool to support lobbyists' integrity, but problems of consistency and interpretation may arise where lobbyists are subject to more than one code. It is therefore essential to:

- Improve the standards and guidelines associated with the range of actions that can influence public policy, to ensure that lobbyists' engagement does not raise issues of integrity and inclusiveness in public policy processes.
- Introduce more detailed integrity standards to specify the due diligence requirements that companies, organisations and the associations in which they participate, must meet to ensure alignment between with public affairs and sustainability agendas.

Quebec could strengthen the ethical framework for interest representatives

In Quebec, the Lobbying Transparency and Ethics Act is accompanied by a Code of Conduct for Lobbyists that establishes standards of conduct applicable to lobbyists in order to ensure the proper exercise of lobbying activities and to promote transparency. Of the 38 jurisdictions that responded to the OECD 2020 Survey on Lobbying, 17 have introduced similar codes originating in law (OECD, 2021[2]). In general, these codes represent the minimum expectations that society places on interest representatives.

In its Statement of Principles, the Quebec Commissioner of Lobbying recommends establishing an ethical framework applicable to entities and interest representatives for the disclosure, carrying out and follow-up of lobbying activities in a way that maintains the highest standards of integrity and professionalism and promotes citizens' trust in public institutions (Principle 11 of the Statement of Principles). The Commission also recommends assigning the interest representative and the entity for which they are an administrator, associate, officer, employee or member the joint responsibility of ensuring compliance with the ethical framework for the interest representative in carrying out lobbying activities (Principle 12 of the Statement of Principles).

The responsibility would no longer rest solely with the individual carrying out the lobbying activities, but would also be linked to the entity on whose behalf the activities are carried out. Thus, the company or organisation will be responsible for compliance with the framework by its internal representatives, while the firm of external representatives will be responsible for the individuals attached to it. This introduces the clear responsibility of firms towards the people they employ and their managers. The Quebec Commission of Lobbying believes that this will encourage entities to adopt internal compliance rules, thereby raising the degree of professionalism with which lobbying activities should be carried out, but also encouraging representatives to be more cautious since they expose themselves not only to external sanctions, under the legislative regime for example, but also to internal sanctions.

Quebec could encourage businesses and interest representatives to go beyond an interpretation related to the Lobbying Transparency and Ethics Act

Although lobbying is an essential tool for engaging with public decision-makers, it is not the only method used by companies to influence the policy-making process. For example, they can channel their influence by funding political parties or election campaigns, or by funding research or think tanks to generate knowledge and ideas on particular policy issues.

As with lobbying, the use of such alternative or complementary measures to engage in policy-making is legitimate and can help inform the policy-making process. However, the funding of political parties or election campaigns that exploit legal loopholes (OECD, 2016[11]), or the funding of think tanks or research groups to manipulate data or evidence, is a clear violation of the principles of integrity (OECD, 2021[2]). In companies with inadequate internal governance standards, unconstrained activities to influence policy-making processes, whether directly or indirectly, can have serious repercussions and raise concerns among shareholders, investors and consumers. Indeed, large institutional investors are becoming increasingly aware of the financial and non-financial risk of malpractice and are facing more pressure; as a result, risk and crisis management has become more dominant and the demand for transparency has increased.

Quebec could therefore consider encouraging companies and organisations to establish standards that specify how to ensure integrity in these methods of influence. Standards could cover issues such as ensuring accuracy and plurality of views, promoting transparency in the funding of research organisations and think tanks, and managing and preventing conflicts of interest in the research process. Also, setting clear standards for companies in the provision of data and evidence could help ensure integrity in decision-making. These standards could also specify voluntary disclosures that may involve social responsibility considerations regarding a company's involvement in public policy-making and lobbying (Box 3.6).

Box 3.6. Responsible lobbying standards and due diligence requirements on lobbying and trade association alignment

To better understand how they address corporate political engagement risks, investors can also encourage companies to formalise responsible engagement standards and internal processes that address the full scope of corporate and trade association conduct in the policy-making process. The standards and processes could cover the following areas:

- Explaining how lobbying and influence activities align with public commitments to support goals on climate change and other shared sustainability challenges.
- Establishing adequate due diligence measures to ensure that the positions and practices of those who lobby on a company's behalf (industry and lobby associations) do not run afoul of the organisation's values and commitments. This may include:
    - Processes to regularly review membership of trade associations and third-party organisations and identify misalignment.
    - Transparency on memberships of trade associations or other third-party organisations that may engage in political activities (charities, foundations, PACs, fundraising organisations).
    - The level of funding and engagement in these organisations (e.g. representation on the board, funding beyond membership, participation in specific committees or working groups).
    - Actions taken when the positions and lobbying practices of these organisations do not align with the company's own lobbying practices and commitments.
- Mainstreaming these standards across all business lines – including government affairs and sustainability functions to create a coherent position across the company's government affairs activities and CSR/ESG branches. These policies should ensure that CSR/ESG teams have sufficient access to information on a company's lobbying activities and trade association membership.
- Adopting transparency and integrity measures on the hiring of former public officials.
- Specifying the role of board members, top management and senior executives in regularly monitoring the implementation of the standards.
- Ensuring that employees have the knowledge and capacity to implement the standards in their daily work.

Source: (OECD/PRI, 2022[12]).

Proposals for action

In order to foster a culture of integrity in interactions between lobbyists and public officials, and to be as consistent as possible with international best practice, the OECD recommends that Quebec consider the following proposals.

Strengthening the integrity framework for public officials

- Clarify and, if necessary, establish or strengthen specific integrity standards for public officials and the behaviour expected from lobbying activities.
- Clarify the responsibility of public officials to enforce the Lobbying Transparency and Ethics Act.
- Strengthen the rules before, during and after a public mandate.
- Build the capacity of ethics advisors to prepare them to answer questions from public officials related to the Act and the risks associated with lobbying practices.

Promoting responsible engagement by lobbyists

- Quebec could strengthen the ethical framework applicable to interest representatives.
- Quebec could encourage businesses and interest representatives to go beyond an interpretation related to the Lobbying Transparency and Ethics Act.

References

Faccio, M. (2006), "Politically connected firms", *American Economic Review*, Vol. 96/1, pp. 369-386, http://www.jstor.org/stable/30034371 (accessed on 30 December 2014). [5]

Lobbyisme Québec (2021), *Mémoire présenté à la commission parlementaire concernant le Projet de loi n°49 – Loi modifiant la Loi sur les élections et les référendums dans les municipalités, la Loi sur l'éthique et la déontologie en matière municipale*, https://lobbyisme.quebec/wp-content/uploads/2021/07/memoire-pl-49.pdf. [8]

Lobbyisme Québec (2019), *Simplicité, Clarté, Pertinence, Efficacité. Réforme de l'encadrement du lobbyisme*, https://www.commissairelobby.qc.ca/fileadmin/Centre_de_documentation/Documentation_institutionnelle/2019-06-13_Enonce-principes-CLQ.pdf. [3]

Lobbyisme Québec (2010), *Mémoire présenté en entendu en commission parlementaire concernant le Projet de loi n° 109 – Loi sur l'éthique et la déontologie en matière municipale à la suite de l'étude détaillée faite par la Commission sur l'aménagement du territoire*, https://lobbyisme.quebec/wp-content/uploads/2021/07/MVmoire_CLQ_projet_de_loi_no_109.pdf. [7]

Lobbyisme Québec (2009), *Mémoire présenté et entendu en commission parlementaire concernant le Projet de loi n°76 – Loi modifiant diverses dispositions législatives concernant principalement le processus d'attribution des contrats des organismes municipaux*, https://lobbyisme.quebec/wp-content/uploads/2021/07/Memoire_CLQ_projet_de_loi_no_76.pdf. [6]

OECD (2021), *Lobbying in the 21st Century: Transparency, Integrity and Access*, OECD Publishing, Paris, https://doi.org/10.1787/c6d8eff8-en. [2]

OECD (2020), *OECD Public Integrity Handbook*, OECD Publishing, Paris, https://doi.org/10.1787/ac8ed8e8-en. [9]

OECD (2016), *Financing Democracy: Funding of Political Parties and Election Campaigns and the Risk of Policy Capture*, OECD Publishing, Paris,, https://doi.org/10.1787/9789264249455-en. [11]

OECD (2009), *Towards a Sound Integrity Framework: Instruments, Processes, Structures and Conditions for Implementation (GOV/PGC/GF(2009)1)*, Organisation for Economic Co-operation and Development, Paris. [10]

OECD/PRI (2022), *Regulating corporate political engagement: trends, challenges and the role for investors*, OECD Publishing, Paris, https://www.oecd.org/governance/ethics/regulating-corporate-political-engagement.htm. [12]

Premier ministre du Canada (2015), *Pour un engagement ouvert et responsable*, https://pm.gc.ca/fr/nouvelles/notes-dinformation/2015/11/27/gouvernement-ouvert-et-responsable. [1]

Yates, S. (2018), "La transparence des activités de lobbyisme au Québec : La grande illusion ?", *Revue française d'administration publique*, Vol. 1/165, pp. 33-47, https://doi.org/10.3917/rfap.165.0033. [4]

Annex A. Statement of Principles of the Québec Commissioner of Lobbying (2019)

PREAMBLE

The proposed lobbying regime should recognise:

A. Everyone must have access to pubic institutions

It is in the public interest for everyone to have access to public institutions in order to participate in their policies and decisions.

B. Submissions of interest contribute to the policies and decisions of public institutions

The submissions made to elected officials, officers and employees of public institutions generally contribute to bringing useful elements of information and understanding into reflection and decision making.

C. Lobbying activities relevant to the public must be transparent

In order to encourage the exercise of citizens' fundamental rights and to maintain their trust in public institutions, the State and public institutions must ensure the transparency of submissions of interest relevant to the public that aim to exercise an influence on the policies or decisions of the institutions and constitute lobbying activities.

D. Transparency and sound practice ensure legitimacy

Transparency and sound practice in lobbying render it legitimate.

E. Transparency is a shared responsibility between all stakeholders

All stakeholders in lobbying activities, including entities and their interest representatives, beneficiaries of the activities and public institutions have the shared responsibility of ensuring transparency for the public's benefit.

F. The regulatory framework must be mandatory and complied with

In order to ensure the transparency of lobbying activities, the State must maintain a mandatory regulatory framework that includes disclosure rules and an ethics framework as well as the powers necessary to ensure compliance.

G. The regulatory framework must be founded on the disclosure of relevant information in a timely manner

The regulatory framework must be founded on the relevance of disclosing lobbying activities so that everyone may be adequately informed in a timely manner.

H. The plan must be adapted to the reality of both activities and institutions

The regulatory framework must be adapted to the reality of lobbying different levels of public institutions and be in accordance with the nature of those lobbying activities.

I. The regulatory framework must be simple, clear and consistent with its environment

In the spirit of simplicity, clarity, relevance and efficiency, the framework must be consistent with others dealing with transparency and integrity put in place by public institutions.

J. The State must ensure a space for open and fair dialogue with its citizens

The State must maintain a space for fair and accessible dialogue with its citizens and, to this end, the lobbying framework must not wrongfully restrict access to public institutions.

Scope of the Act

1. Activities are clearly defined and target policies or decisions relevant to the public

Define the following as lobbying activities relevant to the public and require their disclosure:
- Any intervention, either direct or through an intermediary, with a public institution, whose goal is
- To suggest or change the development, content, drafting or implementation of any type of legislative, regulatory, strategic or administrative policy; or
- To influence the decision-making process of a public institution concerning any financial investment, contract, permit or other authorization determined by the Act or by regulation, or the appointment of any person holding a key position within the State.

2. The Act regulates grassroots lobbying

Regulate grassroots lobbying activities.

3. The framework must be adjusted by regulation according to the institutions and activities covered

By regulation, establish specific, adapted rules concerning the regulation and disclosure of certain lobbying activities towards different levels of public institutions, especially concerning any form of financial investment, contract, permit or other form of authorization that it is relevant to regulate.

4. The Act covers all relevant interest representatives

Regulate lobbying activities exercised by all interest representatives acting on behalf of an individual or entity, regardless of its nature, including a grouping of entities.

5. No minimum threshold of activity is required, nor do interest representatives need to be remunerated for the Act to apply

No minimum threshold of activity is required, nor do interest representatives need to be remunerated for the Act to apply.

6. All public institutions and their representatives are covered by the Act

Cover all public institutions and the elected officials, officers and employees of those institutions that lobbying activities may be directed towards, including the legislative, executive and administrative systems at the provincial and municipal levels.

7. The Act ensures a space for dialogue with public institutions

Exclude submissions of interest made without an intermediary:
- by an individual or group of individuals to promote their own rights or interests as citizens or taxpayers of the State.
- by an entity, in its role as citizen or taxpayer of the State, to promote its own rights or interests if its intervention is specifically provided for or required by law and carried out in accordance with specific processes.
- by a community organization primarily offering support services directly to the public.

Responsibilities and obligations in lobbying activities

8. An individual or entity must be registered in order to carry out an activity

Require all individuals and entities to register in the disclosure system established by the Act if they wish to carry out lobbying activities with or without an intermediary.

9. Entities are responsible for authorizing intermediaries to undertake lobbying activities on their behalf

Assign the represented entities the responsibility of authorizing any interest representative to carry out lobbying activities on its behalf and of ensuring the disclosure, truthfulness, reliability and follow-up of lobbying activities performed by their in-house interest representatives.

10. Entities can delegate responsibilities to external representatives

Assign external interest representatives the responsibility of ensuring the disclosure, truthfulness, reliability and follow-up of lobbying activities made on behalf of their clients.

11. Lobbying activities must be subject to ethical principles and obligations of conduct

Establish an ethical framework applicable to entities and interest representatives for the disclosure, carrying out and follow-up of lobbying activities in a way that maintains the highest standards of integrity and professionalism and promotes citizens' trust in public institutions.

12. Entities and their representatives are jointly responsible for compliance with the Act

Assign the interest representative and the entity for which they are an administrator, associate, officer, employee or member the joint responsibility of ensuring compliance with the ethical framework for the interest representative in carrying out lobbying activities.

13. Regulations prescribe requirements on keeping information relevant to the activities

By regulation, prescribe the requirements for keeping information on lobbying activities for verification and inquiry purposes.

14. All public institutions must designate a reference person for the application of the Act

Designate the primary officer of any public institution or any person within that institution to whom the officer will delegate the responsibility as reference person for the application of and compliance with the Act within the institution.

15. The framework establishes ethical principles and obligations of conduct during and after the terms of office of elected officials and certain officers from public institutions

Establish disclosure and confidentiality obligations, an ethical framework and specific prohibitions applicable to lobbying activities undertaken by elected officials or officers designated by public institutions during and after the end of their term or duties for the public institutions with which they had or maintained connections or official relations. The framework must also allow the Commissioner of lobbying to grant a full or partial exemption from such obligations, rules or prohibitions when doing so is not contrary to the spirit of the Act.

Disclosure regime

16. The disclosure system is efficient and open, providing access to the relevant information in a timely manner

Establish a mandatory, public disclosure system for lobbying activities based on open data and providing free access, at all times, to relevant and verifiable information allowing anyone to be aware of and understand the lobbying activities and respond to them in a timely manner.

17. All relevant information must be disclosed

Require all relevant information to be disclosed, including the identity of interest representatives and entities undertaking or benefiting from lobbying activities, public institutions targeted and all information, financial or otherwise, that is deemed relevant for understanding the goals of a lobbying activity and the means used to carry it out.

18. The Act confers the responsibility for the plan on the Commissioner of lobbying

Confer the responsibility and administration of the disclosure system on the Commissioner of lobbying.

19. The Act must require disclosure of intent and follow-up for lobbying activities

Require the disclosure of any intention to undertake lobbying activities and the follow-up of any activity undertaken, especially if an elected official or an officer designated by a public institution is being lobbied.

20. Organizations may disclose the entirety of the activities carried out by their members

Allow an entity to disclose, for a specific mandate, the entirety of the lobbying activities undertaken by the individuals or entities that are its members, by assuming, on their behalf, the responsibility for and conformity of the lobbying activities.

Legislative compliance, responsibilities, powers and duties

21. The lobbying framework is under the jurisdiction of the National Assembly

Confirm that the framework for lobbying public institutions is under the authority of the National Assembly and maintain the Commissioner of lobbying's responsibilities as the person designated to perform the functions provided for in the Act.

22. The Commissioner of lobbying acts independently in accordance with his or her powers and duties

Set out the Commissioner of lobbying's duties in a way that ensures impartiality, independence of action and fairness of decisions, and set out the establishment by the National Assembly of the Commissioner's powers, the appointment, replacement and remuneration procedure as well as the method of financing and accountability for activities.

23. The Commissioner of lobbying's powers and duties are consistent with those of other designated persons

Set out the powers and duties for the Commissioner of lobbying that are adapted to the position and consistent with those of other persons designated by the National Assembly.

24. The Act provides for a range of powers necessary for the plan's application

For the Commissioner of lobbying and the persons the Commissioner designates, maintain the powers and protection for commissioners appointed under the Act respecting public inquiry commissions as well as the powers of inquiry, verification and inspection, and introduce the power to make formal demands to provide information as well as the power to publish certain reports and recommendations or penalties when deemed relevant for the purposes of the Act.

25. Penalties imposed are proportional and adapted to the offences

Maintain penal and disciplinary penalties and introduce monetary administrative penalties that are proportional and adapted to the nature and seriousness of the offences, allowing for a sliding scale of penalties and their publication if deemed relevant for the purposes of the Act.

26. Mandatory training can be imposed as a disciplinary penalty

Grant the Commissioner, as part of disciplinary powers, the capacity to impose mandatory training on any interest representative.

27. Prescription periods must be consistent

Establish a prescription regime adapted to the nature of the offences provided for by the Act and consistent with similar existing regimes in Québec.

28. The Commissioner may issue notices, orders or exemptions

Set out the Commissioner's power to issue guidelines, orders and interpretive notices covering interpretation, application and compliance with the Act, as well as the power to exempt the publication of information related to lobbying activities if its disclosure may be prejudicial to an individual, entity or public institution.

29. The Act allows recommendations to be issued

Grant the Commissioner the power to issue recommendations to a public institution, interest representative or any other individual or entity in order to ensure that the Act and its ethical principles and obligations of conduct are respected.

30. The Commissioner's mission includes an educational portion

Introduce an educational mission specifically for the Commissioner of lobbying and the obligation to offer public institutions, interest representatives and citizens a program and tools for training and education on the regulatory framework established by the Act.

31. A training program is introduced for all stakeholders

Introduce a training program for elected officials and officers designated by public institutions, continuing education for external interest representatives and the responsibility for all registered entities to offer such training to their in-house interest representatives.

32. A regulatory power, subject to the National Assembly's approval, allows the Act to be adapted as needed

Set out a regulatory power, subject to the National Assembly's approval, for efficiently adapting and developing the legislative framework according to societal expectations and best practices concerning the lobbying activities' framework.

33. The National Assembly may assign other powers and duties to the Commissioner of lobbying

Set out, for the Commissioner of lobbying, any other duty, power or function that the National Assembly deems necessary to ensure the Act is complied with.

34. A revision and consultation process allows the framework to evolve

Establish a regular, mandatory process for the Act's revision as well as a submission and consultation mechanism allowing the Commissioner to formulate, in a timely manner, recommendations to a committee or any other appropriate authority under the jurisdiction of the National Assembly.